The Rats Are in the Cheese

Visit www.booksurge.com to order additional copies.

JON ZAGRODZKY
ILLUSTRATED BY GARY MILLER

THE RATS ARE IN THE CHEESE
One Hedgehog's Political Journey

2007

The Rats Are in the Cheese

"Everything should be made as simple as possible, but not simpler."

—*Albert Einstein*

THANK YOU

To my loving wife and best friend, **Sara Zagrodzky**, thank you for support. You gave up many hours we would otherwise have spent together while I wrote this book. I am truly grateful, and I will make it up to you.

To my dear mother, **Phyllis Zagrodzky**, the most patient and capable teacher I know, thank you for teaching me how to write. I'm sure this work is not up to your standards despite my best efforts, but I hope it's close.

To **Gary Miller**, a remarkable cartoon talent, thank you for allowing me to benefit from your wonderful gifts. Your drawings have brought this story to life in ways that mere words never could.

To **Jack Murrin**, my boss and an exceptionally capable individual, thank you for the many helpful legal and editorial contacts you provided to me, as well as for your wise advice and counsel.

To my children, **Maggie** and **Jack,** yes we can go to the beach and play ball now.

This book is dedicated to my father
Russell Edward (Ed) Zagrodzky

Even as a young child, I remember how passionate my dad was about public policy. I can recall him sitting me down as an eleven-year-old to watch Richard Nixon's resignation speech, encouraging me to read the paper every day, and taking the time to explain political ideas and events. In time, I developed many of these same passions, which I hope to pass on to my children.

My dad helped shape many of the ideas in this book. Over the past two years, I spent countless hours with him debating various approaches to tax reform. His curiosity, experience, intellect, and creativity proved extremely valuable.

Beyond his help on this book, the most important thing about my dad is, well, that he's my dad. I am truly grateful for the many lessons he has imparted to me over the years. Thanks, Dad.

If everyone had a dad like mine, the world would be a better place.

AUTHOR'S NOTE

In 1944, George Orwell published <u>Animal Farm</u>, an allegorical novel he wrote to criticize the hypocrisy of the Soviet Union.

In his novel, animals rise up to wrest control of a farm from Mr. Jones, a drunkard who mistreated and neglected the animals. Once in charge, the animals began work to create a more just society. "All animals are equal," among other slogans, became the basis by which the animals governed themselves.

Over time, though, these ideals were corrupted, and the animals succumbed to the same tyranny that plagued them under Farmer Jones. Like the Soviet Union, the promises of equality and prosperity never materialized. "All animals are equal" became "all animals are equal, but some animals are more equal than others," a brilliant twisting of words by Orwell that most people recall even now.

Orwell did us a great favor by cleverly exposing the Soviet state for what it was. All these years later, however, the lessons of <u>Animal Farm</u> seem quaint and almost irrelevant. After all, America prevailed in its long struggle against the Soviets, relegating them to the "ash heap of history," as one U.S. president put it. Today, we can take great comfort that tyranny remains absent from our society.

Or can we?

PREFACE

*I*t was a cool and pleasant evening.

A hedgehog had just stirred from his day-long slumber. Not willingly, though. He just wasn't an "evening hedgehog" like most hedgehogs were. If his stomach hadn't been grumbling, he might have just skipped getting up altogether.

"Time for dinner," he muttered, half asleep. He rolled over lazily, not too happy about that fact. It took a couple of minutes, but he finally staggered to his feet. As he lumbered out of his den, he stumbled and fell flat on his face.

What a klutz, he thought. *How can someone as low to the ground as I am stumble and fall like that? Maybe I should just go back to bed.* But the only thing a hedgehog hates more than being tired, or klutzy for that matter, is being hungry.

As he stepped outside, he quickly perked up. It was truly a cool and pleasant evening.

I'll bet there's no shortage of dinnertime goodies crawling around, he thought as the cool night air awakened his senses. *Bugs just love evenings like this, and I just love bugs.*

He began to make his way slowly to a spot where he knew they'd be crawling around in abundance. *I'm sure glad bugs are so unaware of what's going on around them. They never sense that I'm coming. Once I find them, dinner is a snap.*

One might say the same about the hedgehog himself. Well, maybe not that last part.

***

As it turned out, hedgehogs weren't the only creatures in the forest known to wake up hungry after sundown.

Not far from the hedgehog's den, a handsome fox awakened in his lair feeling the same hunger pangs as the hedgehog. A lot more willing to get up, the fox was on his feet quickly. With grace and speed, he bounded out of his den and began to survey his surroundings.

Time to eat, he thought as he licked his lips with anticipation. *This nice, cool air is going to make dinner an easy catch. All the tasty creatures I like move just a little more slowly when it's cool outside.*

The wily fox wasted no time in starting his search for dinner. With perfect precision, he scampered through the forest, focusing his eyes, ears, and nose on the hunt. The plodding hedgehog, who still hadn't found his own dinner, continued ambling along in a noisy fashion, daydreaming about bugs.

After several minutes, the fox came upon the hedgehog, having heard his dinner guest rustling a minute or so before he actually found him. Ever so silently, he slipped behind some bushes just out of the hedgehog's view.

Frankly, the fox could have made all the noise he wanted; it was not clear that the hedgehog would have sensed anything coming. Not only was the hedgehog a little hard of hearing, but his habit of daydreaming meant that even the most obvious things escaped his attention.

I can't believe I've found dinner already, thought the fox. *This is too easy. That hedgehog doesn't suspect a thing. Just a minute or so more, and he'll be out in the open. That's when I'll make my move. I hear dinner bells already!*

The hedgehog, oblivious to the danger lurking nearby, continued on his way.

You know, the hedgehog pondered to himself, *bugs come in such variety. Even though I eat them every day, it's a different culinary experience each time.*

As the hedgehog approached the clearing, the fox moved in for the kill. His muscles tensed. His heartbeat quickened. His sharp eyes focused directly ahead.

Actually, I live for bug variety, continued the hedgehog to himself. *In fact, I'll bet that all this variety is good for me. Didn't I hear that a diet with lots of variety is healthy?*

It happened so quickly.

In a flash, the fox leapt into the air, zeroing in on dinner with the precision of a dive bomber. For all his inattention, the hedgehog managed to catch what was happening out of the corner of his eye.

"Incoming!" he exclaimed. Instantly, his reflexes took over and he snapped into the shape of a ball, his sharp spines protruding out in every direction.

Oh, oh, thought the fox in midair. *This is really going to hurt!* With that, he landed squarely on the hedgehog.

"Ouch!" cried the fox as a few of the spines pricked his torso. Leaves and dirt flying, the fox and the hedgehog separated, the fox quickly recovering for a counterattack.

"You're not getting away from me," he warned. "I didn't stalk you all this time only to come away empty-handed!" The hedgehog said nothing and remained in his spiny ball.

Still determined, but a bit more tentative, the fox batted the hedgehog around with his paws, hoping to find an opening. Surely there was one! Dinner was right there; he could taste it! "Come on, open up!" No luck.

"Time for more effective measures!" he snarled. He pinned down the hedgehog, opened his mouth wide, and tried to bite his way through the spines.

"Ouch!" cried the fox again, quickly retreating. One of the hedgehog's spines had broken off in the fox's mouth. Not a pretty sight. A little bloody, actually.

Almost as soon as their struggle started, it was over. The frustrated fox circled back and snarled a few more times but was now well aware that he would never get past the hedgehog's spines.

After a few minutes, the hedgehog peeked out. Seeing that the danger had passed, he unrolled from his spiny ball. *Wow*, he thought. *I lost some of my spines that time. Oh well.*

He took a few minutes to stretch and shake off the leaves and dirt. "Those foxes," muttered the hedgehog as he resumed his stroll. "They don't get any smarter; they just get louder."

He kept thinking as he walked along. *Dad was right. "Hedgies" are great. Being able to snap into one like that has always kept me safe from the fox. They're automatic, and they keep bad things from happening.*

Just then, the spot he'd been searching for appeared as he came around a large tree.

"Ah," he exclaimed. "It's dinnertime! And just look at the incredible variety of bugs! Didn't I hear that a diet with lots of variety is healthy?"

I

Napoleon was dead.

The dreadful tyrant who had ruled Animal Farm for years had finally succumbed to gluttony and alcoholism. It wasn't a complete surprise, though, since rumors had been circulating for months that his health was failing and that he might meet his demise any day.

According to unofficial accounts, he spent his last weeks sprawled on an enormous bed in the old farm house. Surrounded by opulence, he passed the time ordering others to move furniture around, rearrange flowers, and fan him vigorously whenever he felt too warm. No indulgence was refused.

Soon, it became clear that death might come any day. Napoleon sent for his closest friends, other pigs actually, to come to his bedside. Within an hour of doing so, several of them had arrived, filling the room to capacity. Together with Napoleon, those pigs had become the elite ruling class on the farm, entitling them to luxuries other animals could only imagine. It was clear that none of those pigs had missed any meals.

Eventually, the end did come, but it was a painfully slow process. Napoleon spent his final hours recounting, yet again, the sacrifices he had endured to lead Animal Farm. Coughing and wheezing, the old boar spoke at length about the great battles he had led against Farmer Jones and about the utopian society these battles had ushered in. Currying favor to the end, his friends offered lavish praise each time he paused to take a breath. One went so far as to promise that the other animals on the farm would spare no effort or expense in memorializing Napoleon's legacy.

Finally, in the middle of a sentence extolling the virtues of his leadership, Napoleon expired with one last loud and rumbling exhale, filling the room with an odor so awful that it instantly wilted the leaves of every nearby plant. Escape from the deadly fumes quickly became a priority for everyone, with pigs bolting for the door all at once in a stampede that nearly resulted in additional fatalities.

Within an hour or so, farm criers began spreading the news. As the other animals learned what had happened, they wailed and moaned loudly, particularly when pigs or any of Napoleon's dogs were watching. In private, though, they rejoiced, for the tyrant that had lorded over them for so long had finally died.

Not that any of this really mattered. For quite some time, animals had been fleeing the farm, fed up with the hunger and misery. Some simply moved to other farms, but others decided to start new societies, vowing not to repeat the mistakes that had led to the failure of Animal Farm.

One particularly determined group was a band of small animals. Tired of the dreadful living conditions and being stepped on all too frequently, especially by the horses, a number of these feisty little creatures decided that enough was enough and began planning their own escape to freedom.

The scheming and plotting began with a secret late-night meeting, just a month or so after Napoleon's demise. Ever so quietly, several small animals assembled in an old shed, far from the main barn so they wouldn't attract any attention. Despite considerable neglect over the years, the shed was in decent shape. With plenty of straw covering the ground and enough windows to keep it cool, it was a comfortable place.

The meeting came to order quickly. To develop the escape plan as efficiently as possible, the group divided up the planning responsibilities. The hens and roosters worked out the overall escape route. The rabbits, who had been rather adept at wriggling out of their cages when the humans ran the farm, agreed to chew through the back fence to create several escape holes. The clever cats determined that the best time to escape would be early evening after a hot day of field work, when the exhausted animals assigned to late guard duty would be less attentive than usual. Finally, the goats volunteered for communications duty. As the fastest of the small animals, they could keep the group connected and quickly warn everyone in the event of danger.

A few weeks later, the time came to set their escape plans in motion. Late one afternoon, after a long day of field work under a blazing hot sun, the cats realized that the moment was right and signaled the goats to notify everyone. Very carefully, one by one, the animals slipped unnoticed through the newly created fence holes. Once outside the farm, they scurried through an open meadow and were soon on their way to....

Well, they didn't know where they were going, as no one in the group had given any thought to long-range planning. But that hardly seemed important. After all, they were free! Free from tyranny! Free from oppression! Free from being trampled! Truly free!

In fact, their newfound freedom was all they could talk about. As they made their way across the countryside, other animals within earshot overheard the excitement. Soon, a number of these other animals, some from nearby farms and homes and some wild, began to follow the group. Within a few days, the original small group had turned into a crowd, with all sorts of small animals joining the journey to freedom. The newcomers were a diverse group and included rats, mice, squirrels, chipmunks, porcupines, and even a few hedgehogs.

The most interesting animals to join up were the rats. Contrary to what the pigs on Animal Farm told everyone, it turned out that the rats were both intelligent and creative. As the freedom marchers meandered through the countryside, the rats began thinking about what kind of locale would be most appropriate for their new animal society. They interviewed other animals for ideas, ran ahead of the group to scout out possible sites, and talked constantly among themselves about what kind of place they needed.

Soon, the freedom marchers came upon the bank of a slow-moving river. In the middle of the river was a large island, which the rats quickly concluded was the perfect place to start anew.

From the perspective of a small animal, the island was immense almost beyond imagination. In fact, only the animals with the sharpest eyes could see far enough to tell that it was in fact an island and not just the opposite riverbank.

It had every feature an animal could hope for. Plenty of trees and plants covered the landscape, but there were also open spaces, rolling hills, caves, and even a waterfall or two. With such variety, it was clear that animals of every kind would be able to find a home.

What a marvelous find! What a stroke of luck!

With a few days of effort and some rat ingenuity, the animals figured out how to cross the river and get over to the island. Finally, after years of living in oppression, the small animals were free! It was only a matter of time before they sorted out just how to create the society of their dreams. No more tyranny! Long live Freedom Island!

***

One of the original Animal Farm commandments read "all animals are equal." Later on, though, the pigs corrupted these words to their advantage by adding "but some are more equal than others." The change symbolized the unfairness, inequality, and tyranny that eventually overwhelmed Animal Farm.

As they established their new island home, those originally from Animal Farm were particularly mindful of this experience. They made sure that the newcomer animals heard every last detail about the mistreatment, wretchedness, and despair that characterized their prior existence. Before long, every animal came to realize that words such as "some are more equal than others" could easily put their new society on a fast path to tyranny.

Soon, the time came for action. A number of animals began to realize that they had to move beyond talking about how awful Animal Farm was and start thinking about how to prevent a repeat experience on Freedom Island. It wasn't long before animals began discussing what to do next. The real debate didn't start, though, until one of the discussions evolved into something more heated.

One afternoon, in a large clearing on the west side of the island, a goat and a mouse were debating what attributes the Freedom Island government should have. Their debate was wide-ranging, covering not only the form of government but also issues like freedom of speech and limits on government authority. The mouse argued his views with such passion that he attracted the attention of nearby animals, who couldn't help but wonder what all the squeaking was about. After a while, a small crowd had assembled. Tempers began to flare.

Fortunately, several rats saw that matters were getting out of hand and intervened to calm things down. Soon, they managed bring some order to the debate and helped sort out and organize the issues. After several more hours of arguing, Honest Abe Rat, who first spotted the island from the riverbank several months earlier, stepped up onto a large rock in the middle of the clearing to address the crowd.

Honest Abe looked the part. A gray-haired and serious-looking rat with long whiskers, he inspired confidence whenever he spoke. In his short speech, he summarized the key discussion points and offered a draft list of Freedom Island rules for everyone's consideration. To build majority support, he proposed holding full-day debates for each rule, followed by a vote.

Over the next several days, animals argued in a forceful but civil manner. Slowly but surely, Honest Abe edited the rules to reflect the best arguments. He did such a good job at capturing consensus views that each rule received overwhelming support when votes were taken.

Finally, the animals reached full agreement on the basic rules by which they should be governed, which they named the Freedom Rules. To ensure that the new Freedom Rules would be visible to all animals, a few beavers chiseled them onto a wooden plank:

I.   All animals are equal before the law
II. All animals have the right to free speech
III. Animals shall be governed by a Council elected every two years by majority vote
IV. The Council shall be led by an Esteemed Leader who shall also be elected every two years
V.   The Council shall have the ability to pass laws and levy reasonable taxes
VI. The Freedom Rules can be changed only with a two-thirds vote of all animals

(Years later, the animals incorporated the plank into a huge monument, which they placed in the middle of the clearing where the Freedom Rules debate took place. In time, this clearing became the main town square and a popular meeting place for political discourse.)

A few months after the animals agreed on the Freedom Rules, they held the first Esteemed Leader and Council elections. No one really disagreed about who should be elected to the Council, since there was a small but highly visible group of animals that had provided most of the leadership so far. Even the choice of Esteemed Leader was obvious. Honest Abe Rat had clearly earned the position, and the vote to elect him was unanimous.

Honest Abe wasn't the only rat held in high regard. In fact, rats in general had earned considerable respect and deserved much credit for the early success of Freedom Island. Not only did they figure out how to cross the river to get to the island, but they also played a critical role in organizing Freedom Island so that it could function efficiently.

One of the most important initiatives they undertook was to propose a better way for animals to trade with each other. Up to this point, very few animals had much experience with anything resembling money. But the rats realized that some form of money would eventually become necessary.

For a while, no one could agree on what to use for money. A hen suggested using twigs and small sticks, but others rejected her idea because there were too many sticks on the island—everyone would be rich! A turtle proposed using rocks, but the mice turned down that idea because rocks were too heavy for them.

One night, as a number of animals found themselves engaged in yet another debate about money, several rats started feeling hungry, so they broke out a ration of their favorite food, cheese. No one took notice until the cheese's wonderful smell filled the air. Soon, the animals stopped what they were doing to enjoy the aroma.

In those few moments of quiet sniffing, one clever rat startled everyone with the suggestion to use cheese as currency. At first the idea was rejected, but soon the animals admitted that cheese had a number of desirable characteristics—it was lightweight, reasonably challenging to make in large quantities, easily stored, and highly desirable. Soon, everyone warmed to the idea of cheese as money, especially animals with poor eyesight but a keen sense of smell. Several rats proposed the new money system to the recently elected Council, which approved the plan unanimously.

As small animals reproduce themselves quickly, Freedom Island transformed itself into a populous and vibrant society in a short period, eventually becoming the envy of other communities along the river. The wisdom embedded by Honest Abe and the other founders in the Freedom Rules allowed the animals to achieve a level of productivity, happiness, and peace that no other animal society had achieved.

No more tyranny! Long live Freedom Island!

***

"Dismissed!" shouted the teacher.

Classes for the day had finally ended, and all the youngsters scurried outside. Leading the way was a group of lemmings, who might have led the others down the road and into the river if parents and family friends had not been waiting outside to stop them.

Hedge was never one to charge out of class at the end of the day. Not that he didn't want to, of course. Hedgehogs just weren't endowed with any natural speed, or even very long legs.

Mature beyond his years, Hedge was a serious youth and studied hard. He always looked his best and might have been mistaken for a teacher if he had been just a little bigger.

Fortunately, Hedge lived nearby and could simply walk home by himself after class. Gathering up his things, he made his way outside, well behind the other children. Soon, he was meandering down the path home, lost in thought about the day's lessons.

Many years had passed since the founding of Freedom Island. Over this time, the animals made significant progress, developing a robust economy and establishing some trappings of a modern society. Modest homes, simple businesses, and even schools became commonplace across the island.

"Hi, Mom," shouted Hedge as he arrived home. "I'm going to go study. I have a lot of reading to do."

"Mister, you get in here and give your mother a hug," replied his mother. A cheerful and generous hedgehog, Hedge's mother spared no love for her offspring.

"Yes, Mom," sighed Hedge. For all his protests, he deeply loved his mother. It was just that the hugging was a little too much. After all, they were hedgehogs, and all those spines made hugging a painful experience. Kissing was even worse.

Hedge, once again, survived his mother's excessive attention and finally made it to his room, where he began to study in earnest. After a few hours, he heard someone rustling outside. Quickly realizing who it was, he scurried outside as fast as his short legs would permit.

Hedge's father had a good job as a worker down by the riverbank. Most of his duties entailed clearing brush and weeds, which was physically demanding and tiring. But his employer paid him well, and he had no trouble supporting his family.

Hedge ran to meet his father, who had just arrived home after a long day at work. As usual, he brought home a bag of cheese, his wages for the day. Hedge always liked to see how much cheese his father had.

The family ate some of the cheese and stored the rest as savings. Well, that's not quite true. There were taxes to pay, of course, and Tax Rat came by monthly to collect. Over time, rats ended up filling most of the government and administrative jobs on Freedom Island. Tax Rat had been a tax collector for many years.

"Is he here yet?" inquired Hedge's father, referring to Tax Rat, who almost always came by late in the afternoon on the appointed tax collection day.

"You just missed him," replied Hedge. "Mom paid the cheese tax out of storage."

"Darn," said Hedge's father as he walked indoors and sat down. "I was hoping to see if Tax could stay for dinner. He's a lot of fun to have around. So, how was your day at school?"

"Today, we started learning about Animal Farm," said Hedge.

"Animal Farm?" said Hedge's father. "It's a sad but important story. What do you think so far?"

"Well," replied Hedge, "I think I have a pretty good understanding of what happened, but what I don't understand is why the animals failed to create a better society. I mean, they had everything going for them."

"That's a good question, Hedge," replied his father. "If you ask me, the reason they failed is because they allowed their leaders to change and corrupt their basic commandments. As a result, those leaders ended up trampling on fundamental rights, stifling debate, and crushing freedom. What's worse, as Animal Farm declined and life grew increasingly miserable, they lied about what was happening."

"It sounds awful," replied Hedge.

"It was," said his father leaning back in his chair. "Tyranny, corruption, and mistreatment were commonplace. Sadly, by the time the animals realized that things had gone wrong, the pigs had become too corrupt and too powerful to confront."

"Couldn't the same thing happen to us?" inquired Hedge.

"No way," replied his father. "When our ancestors fled Animal Farm many decades ago, they vowed not to make the same mistakes. They developed a better set of rules and system of government so that the corruption that doomed Animal Farm would never be repeated."

"Never?" inquired Hedge.

"Well, not so far," replied his father, laughing. "But Freedom Island has prospered as a free society for many years, and it's thanks to our Freedom Rules. How many times have you walked by the monument in the town square, where our Freedom Rules are carefully etched in wood? Not one of these rules has changed in all these years because our founders had such good judgment."

"I suppose that's true," said Hedge.

"Of course it is!" exclaimed his father. "Consider what we have today—an efficient and effective government, very little bureaucracy and very low taxes. How much cheese did Mom have to give Tax Rat today? Hardly any, I'll bet."

"You're right, as usual," said Hedge, smiling at his father's enthusiasm.

"Why, just last week I had lunch with our Council representative," continued his father. "She told me about some of the Council's work and asked for my opinion. It was terrific. In fact, I've always felt that on Freedom Island, my voice and my vote count. No one on Animal Farm could have said that."

Hedge's father paused then rose from his chair.

"The last line of our island anthem certainly sums it all up for me," he said proudly. "It makes my spines tingle every time I hear it!"

He took a deep breath and sang the line. He was loud and off-key, but well-meaning.

"No more tyranny! Long live Freedom Island!"

"I think I understand, now," beamed Hedge. "We're really fortunate to live in such a wonderful society. I can't wait until I'm old enough to participate myself!"

"Maybe one day you'll have a chance to serve on the Council," said his father. "Wouldn't that be great?"

"It sure would!" shouted Hedge with excitement.

Later that night, as Hedge slept soundly, he dreamed about Freedom Island. At one point, he saw himself in front of a huge crowd in the town square. Just as the sun was setting, he stepped up onto a platform in front of the Freedom Rules monument. Before him, thousands of animals cheered enthusiastically. A feeling of pride welled up in Hedge like he had never felt before.

"Hedge," said a voice behind him on the platform. Startled out of his slumber, Hedge sat bolt upright, his heart pounding, unsure if what he had been dreaming was real. Soon, the quiet and stillness of his bedroom calmed him, and he quickly fell back asleep.

II

Time passes quickly, especially for animals.

Over the years, Hedge had matured into a fine young adult hedgehog. He had many friends in the community, and he was well-liked and well-respected. Very often, Hedge would show up at a meeting or a party, and everyone would know who he was, mostly because it was hard to mistake him for anyone else. There weren't that many hedgehogs around, and even fewer who were as well-groomed as Hedge.

Despite having many friends, Hedge had never become the community leader he dreamed about as a youngster. Instead, he found himself the owner of a small but modestly successful store that specialized in providing basic necessities.

Freedom Island continued to grow and prosper. Overall, the Council seemed to manage the growth adequately, but some problems were beginning to surface. One of the more serious problems involved a Council member caught up in an ethics scandal, the first time such a thing had ever happened. Apparently, someone tried to bribe the Council member with cheese in exchange for his support on some important new rules being developed.

Talky Beaver, the best known reporter on the island, shocked the public when he uncovered the scheme. But, fortunately, justice was served. Voters turned the scoundrel out of office, and he left the island in disgrace. Public outcry died down soon thereafter, and the Council quickly regained its footing. Everything seemed to get back to normal. Well, at least for a while.

Several months later, a group of animals brought before the Council a proposed project to invest in some rafts and a new river dock, which would help improve trade with other river communities. The project was going to require many workers, and in order to pay these workers their cheese wages, the Council was going to have to raise taxes considerably. A number of Council members were nervous about making such a major decision without broader input, so the Council decided to postpone action until after an upcoming election. That way, the population at large would have ample time to understand the proposal, offer advice to sitting Council members, and express their desires in an informed manner at the ballot box.

As the public started to debate the merits of the proposed project, animals began to take sides. One group favored these kinds of Council-supported investments and the taxes required to pay for them, but another group clearly did not. As a result, the Council races that year featured competing political groups for the first time. Candidates favoring the project won most of the seats on the Council, so the project went forward.

The rats on the island continued to play an ever-expanding role in the society at large. In addition to filling many important government positions and holding many of the seats on the Council, they emerged as leaders in business matters as well. For a long time, this suited most of the residents on the island, as the rats had largely maintained their reputation for integrity since the days of Honest Abe Rat. In fact, several prominent rats were the ones who proposed and were now leading the river project.

One day, not long after the project got underway, the same industrious reporter who broke the bribery scandal, Talky Beaver, reported that some of the river project employees were managing to get paid without having to show up for work. Talky also discovered that the Council had awarded the project contracts without taking any competitive bids, which meant that the taxpayers paid much more for the project than they should have. Worse still, Talky was able to link both of these scandals directly to individual Council members. According to his daily reports, which everyone on the island read religiously, several Council members from both political groups conspired to push through no-bid contracts benefiting the labor union in exchange for secret cheese payoffs. Once again, the public was shocked, but this time more so. Instead of the scandal involving just one member's behavior, it involved the Council at large.

Some of the contractors and workers went to jail, and several Council members resigned from office or decided not to stand for re-election. The real damage, though, was that for the first time, the public began to doubt the integrity and effectiveness of the Council. In addition, the public began to question the integrity of the rats. Nearly all of the animals involved in the scandal were rats, to the profound dismay of many. It turned out that rats running the river project had become well-connected with rats on the Council and had used these connections to get preferential treatment. Talky suspected that other rats were abusing similar connections to take advantage of other Council-sponsored projects; he just couldn't prove it.

It wasn't long before the Council embarked on a major effort to repair its image. Several Council members introduced plans to prevent these kinds of problems from happening again. Initially, the efforts had a positive effect. But fairly quickly, the flow of bad news resumed.

In the months that followed, many animals began to believe that the Council had "lost its magic," as hardly a week went by without Talky Beaver reporting some story that exposed Council corruption or mismanagement. Whether it was projects going badly, cheese being misspent, or well-connected rats receiving special treatment, the Council seemed to be getting out of control. Deep down, everyone was grateful for Talky's tenacity, and they credited him with saving a lot of cheese.

***

One of Hedge's close friends was Politico Rat. Pol, as his friends called him, had been just as interested in politics as Hedge. Over the years, Pol worked very hard in the community, volunteering for just about every task force and committee imaginable. He labored diligently to build relationships with community leaders, and he knew many Council members.

Pol was full of energy and a fast talker, with a deep, resonating voice that everyone loved. He was a little smaller than Hedge and ordinary in appearance, but he used his paws when he talked, so much so that he frequently knocked over anything that happened to be within arm's length. Whenever he was particularly animated about something, most animals knew to clear the area around him quickly of anything fragile.

Hedge and Pol spent many hours debating and discussing politics. Both were particularly proud of the Freedom Rules and wanted to do everything they could to protect them. They found news about Council corruption and mismanagement deeply distressing.

"You know, this really is outrageous," exclaimed Pol. "I mean, look at these stories about scandal and corruption. I never thought I'd read things like this about *our* Council."

"I hear you," replied Hedge. "I can't believe it either. Of course, there's more going on here than what we read in these stories."

"What do you mean?" asked Pol.

"All this special interest pressure from well-connected rats is driving not only corruption, but also a significant expansion in the size and complexity of Council government," replied Hedge, "and everyone is starting to feel the costs."

"How so?" asked Pol.

"Well, consider what I've experienced as a store owner," continued Hedge. "When I opened up several years ago, everything was pretty simple. There was only one rule I had to follow, which was that I had to keep the place clean. In addition, Tax Rat used to come by only once a month, and I only had to pay one low tax.

"Over the years," Hedge went on, "special interests have convinced the Council to impose all kinds of restrictions and regulations on ordinary animals. In my own case, there are now nearly fifty store owner rules I have to follow. In addition to keeping the place clean, I have to have a pathway of a particular width leading up to the store, all the windows have to be of a certain size, and all of the shelves have to be of a certain height. I also have to have stepstools everywhere so that the smallest animals can reach the top shelves without assistance. It's been really expensive to comply with all of this."

"Wow," said Pol.

"That's not the half of it," continued Hedge. "In addition to all these new rules, my taxes are a lot higher than they used to be. Instead of one low cheese tax, I now pay an income tax, a labor tax, a town tax, a pension tax, a store tax, a property tax, and a river tax. And when I die, my heirs will have to pay a big tax on whatever is left."

Pol shook his head in disbelief.

"Not that long ago," Hedge resumed, "Tax Rat was a great family friend, and it was lots of fun when he came over for dinner. Today, though, I hardly ever see Tax. Instead, I see one of the countless tax collectors he has hired, some of whom I have to deal with almost daily. These new collectors are arrogant and demanding, and they employ all kinds of threats to make sure taxes are paid on time."

"Freedom Island has a lot of legitimate obligations, so higher taxes are probably required to some extent," said Pol. "But reading about Council scandals and hearing your stories about the growing burden of regulations and taxes worries me a lot. I think we're in real trouble."

Hedge and Pol continued their discussion well into the night. Though they were clearly concerned about these problems, they both remained confident in the Freedom Rules and had high hopes that eventually the Council would right itself.

One day, a few months later, Pol came into Hedge's store, brimming with excitement.

"Hedge," he exclaimed as he threw open the door. "I need your help with something!"

"What's up?" asked Hedge. "What can I do for you?"

"I want you to be my campaign manager," replied Pol.

"Campaign manager?" asked Hedge.

"Absolutely," said Pol. "I just heard this morning that Cheesy Pocketsfull Rat is retiring from the Council, and I want to replace him. So, I want to launch my candidacy right away, and I want to announce that you're my campaign manager. What do you say?"

Hedge barely hesitated.

"What a great opportunity!" he cried. "I'd love to! Let's meet tonight and map out a strategy."

"Terrific," said Pol. "I'll stop by later and we'll get started."

Pol turned and headed out of the store. Hedge smiled as he left, thinking about how much fun it was going to be to run the campaign. He even thought about how it might help him get more involved in politics himself, a lifelong dream.

***

"What kind of message do you think will resonate with voters?" asked Hedge. It was late in the day, and Pol had returned to the store to discuss strategy.

"I think the theme has to be good government," replied Pol. "Given all of the scandals we've had, I think voters want a candidate who will promise to clean up the Council."

"That's terrific," said Hedge. "I think voters will go for it. Do you have any competition?"

Hedge and Pol belonged to the Active Party rather than the Limited Party. Both political parties had formed as a result of the great debate involving the river project. Hedge and Pol had always felt that the Council should be active and help animals improve their lives, which was a core philosophy of the Active Party.

"The Limited Party team has yet to announce a candidate, but I'm sure I can beat whomever they choose," said Pol. "The Active Party has always been in the majority, and that will surely continue."

"I think you're right," said Hedge, "but we shouldn't take anything for granted."

"I agree," said Pol. "Let's develop some concrete themes."

With that, the two friends began to sketch out some ideas. They debated what messages would be most effective with the voters and ended up deciding that Pol should position three key promises as the centerpiece of his campaign. Hedge sketched out a campaign poster:

If elected, I promise to:

- **Keep taxes low**
- **Ensure that taxes are spent wisely**
- **End the practice of granting special privileges to well-connected rats**

"What do you think?" said Hedge as he turned to show Pol what he had written.

"Fantastic!" exclaimed Pol. "I think these themes will work really well."

"Here's another idea," said Hedge. "Talky Beaver has long been the toast of Freedom Island for all of his great reporting on corruption and scandals. With themes like these, I'll bet he'd be willing to do some favorable reporting on your candidacy."

"Great idea," said Pol. "I'll see if I can get a meeting with him, hopefully before I announce my candidacy."

"And when do you want to do that?" asked Hedge.

"By the end of the week," replied Pol. "I want to make sure we get in front of the voters before the Limited Party fields a candidate."

"The end of the week?" exclaimed Hedge. "We've got a lot of work to do! Not only do you have to meet with Talky, but we also have to prepare campaign signs, write your announcement speech, and develop a voter outreach strategy."

Hedge and Pol worked ceaselessly over the next several days. Pol met with Talky and prepared his campaign signs, while Hedge drafted Pol's announcement speech and devised an outreach strategy. By the end of the week, everything was ready.

On the morning of the big announcement, Hedge got an early start. Pol had chosen the town square as the venue for his announcement, so Hedge had a lot of work to do to get such a large space organized. By noon, though, he was all set, and crowds began to gather in anticipation of Pol's announcement. Talky Beaver found Pol very impressive when they met earlier in the week, so he made sure to get a seat right up front near the platform, ready to report on the newest Council candidate and his message to the voters.

Once the square had filled to capacity, Pol and Hedge made their way to center stage. The crowds cheered wildly, and it was several minutes before Hedge could even introduce Pol.

Soon, the crowd's applause faded, and Pol was able to start his address.

"My friends," Pol began, "whatever our differences, I think we can all agree on at least one thing. And that one thing is that Freedom Island is the greatest society that animals have ever known."

Applause and a few whistles rang through the square.

"And because we all believe this," he continued, "we must also believe that it is our duty and obligation to protect and strengthen this great society. Unfortunately, over the last several years, we have all witnessed a slow deterioration in the quality, competence, and integrity of our Council. No one likes to hear this, but it's true, and we have to deal with it."

Pol paused as the crowd grew quiet.

"I have a profound love for Freedom Island," he continued, his deep voice rising a bit, "and I want to help restore our government to its earlier greatness. I am therefore announcing my candidacy today for a seat on the Council."

As if on cue, Hedge revealed one of the campaign signs, which contained the three promises. He noticed that Pol had modified the original wording slightly, adding the words "do all I can," which seemed harmless.

If elected, I promise to do all I can to:

- Keep taxes low
- Ensure that taxes are spent wisely
- End the practice of granting special privileges to well-connected rats

"If elected," continued Pol after Hedge stepped back from the sign, "this is my commitment to you, the voters. I promise to do all I can to keep taxes low, ensure that taxes are spent wisely, and end the practice of granting special privileges to well-connected rats."

The crowd jumped to its feet, chanting "Pol Rat—Good Government!" over and over again.

"If you want to see a return to good government, to clean government, to the kind of government our founders envisioned, then please vote for me!" shouted Pol above the crowd.

"Pol Rat—Good Government! Pol Rat—Good Government!"

Pol stepped down from the platform, shaking paws and kissing babies. It was clear that he had the enthusiastic support of everyone gathered.

A few days later, the Limited Party announced its candidate. He was much less well-known than Pol, and no one expected him to prevail in the election. Still, as Hedge had advised, Pol didn't take anything for granted, so he campaigned vigorously. On Election Day, several weeks later, the hard work paid off, and Pol won by a landslide.

That evening, Pol, Hedge, and a big group of supporters gathered for an election night celebration that went on for hours. Talky Beaver was ecstatic and believed that his reporting had helped usher in a new era of good government. In a way, he had become part of the political process, more than just a reporter.

At one point, Hedge handed a broom to Pol, who held it high above his head and shouted to the crowd, "Who wants to see some housecleaning in the Council chambers?"

"We do, we do!" shouted the crowd. "Pol Rat—Good Government! Pol Rat—Good Government! Long live Freedom Island!"

III

The swearing-in ceremony for new Council members was always a fun and festive event.

"I, Politico Rat, do solemnly swear that I will uphold the Freedom Rules and faithfully fulfill my duties as a member of the Council."

Once again, the masses cheered loudly. "Pol Rat—Good Government!"

It wasn't just the excitement of the occasion, of course, but the prospect that Pol would actually succeed at restoring the integrity of the Council, and the entire system of government.

A few days later, Pol and Hedge met in Pol's new office. Hedge was surprised at how sparsely furnished it was. Pol explained that since he had made a promise to the voters to clean up the Council, having a fancy office hardly seemed appropriate.

"Hedge," said Pol as they sat down in some plain wooden chairs, "I need your help again."

"You name it, Pol. I'm happy to help," replied Hedge.

"To get things off to a good start, I'd like to initiate some reform efforts, and I'd like you to organize and lead them," said Pol.

Pol then described the efforts he had in mind.

"We need competitive bidding on all Council-approved projects unless it's an emergency situation," Pol continued. "We also need to attract new contractors to bid on Council projects, and part of each project should be set aside for these new contractors. In addition, we should establish an independent committee to examine each project for any sign of corruption or favoritism."

These initiatives were clearly important, and Pol was grateful that Hedge had agreed to help. After Pol finished spelling out what needed to be done, Hedge stood and began to head out the door. On his way out, he bumped into Business Rat, a powerful local business owner. Biz Rat's father had owned the cleaning service that employed Hedge's father many years ago.

"Hello, Hedge," said Biz.

"How are you, Biz?" said Hedge, a little startled. "What brings you here?"

"Oh, just a little matter to discuss with the newest member of the Council," replied Biz.

Biz quickly made his way past Hedge and into Pol's office, closing the door behind him. Hedge paused briefly, thinking about what he had just witnessed. He thought it odd that one of Pol's first visitors was one of the rats indirectly involved in the river project scandal a while back.

"Oh well, maybe he just wants to mend some political fences," said Hedge to himself. "There's nothing wrong with that."

Hedge didn't give it another thought. There was much work to do, and he needed to focus on the many tasks that awaited him.

Meeting with Biz Rat was an experience like no other. Big, loud, and aggressive, with cheesy suits and a derby hat, Biz could dominate conversations and win arguments against even the sharpest opponents.

Biz made his fortune after inheriting his father's cleaning service, which he expanded to include building and landscaping.

Times weren't always good for Biz. Once, right after he launched a major project, he found himself short on cheese, so much so that he couldn't meet payroll for his employees. Scrambling to avoid bankruptcy, he decided to announce to his employees that, in the interest of their health, he would sponsor a company-wide diet initiative to help everyone lose weight. To accomplish the goal, he convinced them that they should give up their cheese wages for three months, most of which he claimed they would eat anyway. To Biz's delight, everyone was so happy with the resulting weight loss that they simply forgot about the cheese he owed them. The experience convinced Biz that he could talk anyone into anything.

Biz quickly proceeded to make himself comfortable in Pol's office. He was a busy rat, and it was time to do some business.

"So, Biz, what can I do for you?" asked Pol cautiously.

"I'm glad you asked," replied Biz. He began to describe some investments he was planning near a large meadow, which he hoped would create jobs. The plans were indeed attractive, as it appeared that in addition to generating new jobs, they would help revitalize a long-neglected area.

"This sounds great," said Pol. "But I don't understand why you've come to me."

"Well, you see," replied Biz, "I'm not sure the economics of this venture are going to work out. So, just to be safe, I'm hoping you'll help me by securing Council approval for lower cheese taxes on the venture until we get it going. The lower taxes would be temporary, of course."

"Gee, I'm not sure about this," responded Pol, thinking about his pledge to the voters. "I was elected to keep taxes low, to ensure that taxes are spent wisely, and to keep tax cheese away from well-connected rats. No offense, but your proposal fails on all counts."

"Now, Pol," interrupted Biz. "You're not seeing the big picture. The animals who voted for you need these jobs, and we need to revitalize this area. Once completed, the project will generate a lot of new tax revenue, which you can use to benefit your constituents. If you don't help me and this project fails, what will the voters think of you and the Active Party?"

"That's a good point," replied Pol.

"Sure it is," said Biz. "Stop thinking of this as granting privileges to the well-connected. Instead, start thinking of this as a new partnership, wherein we collaborate to make Freedom Island a better place. Together, we can make good things happen. So, what do you say?"

"Perhaps you're right," said Pol. "Your proposal will indeed help many animals. Let me see what I can do."

They shook paws, and Biz left through a side door. Pol contemplated what had happened, still worried about his campaign promise. But then again, Biz was right about those jobs. Besides, helping Biz would attract a lot of support from the business community in the next election. And thanks to all the high-paying union jobs the project would create, labor union leaders would love the idea as well. Soon, Pol stopped worrying.

That evening, Pol had dinner with Talky Beaver, during which he explained the benefits of Biz's meadow project. Talky followed up by publishing a number of favorable reports touting the potential new jobs and wonderful benefits. He might have reported on Biz's behind-the-scenes tax deal, had Pol mentioned it.

Talky's reporting quickly generated strong public support for the project. Though Pol delivered a passionate speech about the project at a Council meeting later that month, public enthusiasm had already made Council support a foregone conclusion. By a unanimous vote, the Council approved the lower tax rates Biz wanted, which they were able to do without much effort since Biz himself drafted the required legislation. Conveniently, the legislation didn't specify or even mention an expiration date for the lower taxes. Instead, the Council agreed during its deliberations that it would revisit the lower taxes once Biz certified that the project was economically sound.

***

It turned out that Pol's appointment with Biz wasn't the last such appointment. In the ensuing months, Pol received countless visitors in his office, all of whom were connected to a seemingly unlimited variety of very demanding special interests.

"Councilmember Pol, nice to meet you," said one visitor. "My name is Fairness Rat. I represent Poor Church Mice, and I need your assistance."

Most animals gasped in amazement upon seeing Fairness Rat for the first time, and Pol was no exception. An energetic rat with spiky hair, she wore wild clothing and lots of necklaces and bracelets, which made loud clanking noises any time she moved. That telltale clanking was often a signal to those who knew Fairness well to make themselves scarce quickly, lest they get caught up in yet another lecture on some intractable social problem. In addition to her unique attire, Fairness was never without her small purple sunglasses, which she claimed were needed to conceal some sort of eye disfigurement, but which others believed were needed to conceal substance-induced dilation of the pupils.

Fairness was a long-time radical. Always marching and protesting, she could be seen at practically any rally carrying signs and shouting slogans. Obsessed with the poor and downtrodden, she was constantly petitioning the Council for more cheese to support poverty programs, none of which ever seemed to work.

"Happy to be of assistance, Fairness," said Pol as Fairness glided into his office. "What can I do for you?"

"Well, as you know," said Fairness, amid much clanking of her bracelets, "the Council has a duty to help the poor, and it hasn't been doing a very good job. We need the Council to approve more cheese for Poor Church Mice, a lot more."

"I hear what you're saying," said Pol, "but I'm not sure the taxpayers will like all this new spending. Besides, we already spend a vast amount of cheese to help Poor Church Mice. Are you really sure that even more spending is the right way to go?"

"Absolutely," responded Fairness emphatically. "In fact, it's a moral imperative. We simply must spend whatever is necessary to give Poor Church Mice a helping hand."

"Well, I'd like to help, but we're already spending so much cheese on so many different things, I'm worried that we'll run out," said Pol.

"Councilmember Pol, with all due respect, that's ridiculous," said Fairness. "There is always plenty of Council cheese."

"I'm just not sure about this," responded Pol. "I was elected to keep taxes low, to ensure that taxes are spent wisely, and to keep tax cheese away from well-connected rats. No offense, but your request fails on all counts."

"Let me put it this way," said Fairness angrily. "The Active Party has always supported help for the poor. It's your duty and obligation to continue this tradition. Am I to understand that you want to break with tradition and deny Poor Church Mice the help they need?"

"No, no, Fairness," responded Pol, trying to calm her down. "I do want to help. Perhaps we can raise the required revenue with a new 'Save Our Community' tax combined with small increases in other taxes."

"Don't do that," replied Fairness abruptly. "Why not simply raise taxes on wealthy animals instead? Besides, they earned all their cheese exploiting Poor Church Mice in the first place."

"The wealthy generate a lot of jobs and investment," said Pol. "I don't want to put them out of business. That would be bad for Freedom Island."

"The wealthy can afford to pay more taxes," insisted Fairness, "and Poor Church Mice need the help. It's as simple as that. I don't know why you're hesitating."

"Let me see what I can do," said Pol.

A few fiery speeches later, as only Pol could deliver, the Council passed additional assistance for Poor Church Mice passed. To pay for it, the Council increased taxes on the wealthy.

***

Another interesting visitor showed up at Pol's office a week after the Poor Church Mice assistance legislation passed.

"Greetings, Councilmember Pol," said the visitor. "The name's Rich Rat. I'd like a few minutes of your time."

Rich Rat was the richest animal on Freedom Island. He had more cheese and owned more land than anyone. Rich earned his name and his fortune thanks to his parents, from whom he inherited a great deal. According to various accounts, Rich's ancestors were the first animals to stake out major property claims on Freedom Island. They were so consumed by this that they were the only animals who didn't witness Honest Abe Rat's inaugural speech as the first Esteemed Leader.

Rich was so rich that he could afford almost unlimited luxuries. Over time, he had assembled a huge staff of attendants and valets who catered to his every whim. One group combed his fur, plucked hairs from his tail (he really hated those hairs), and polished his claws every morning. Another group prepared special meals consisting of exotic cheeses shaped in small cubes and served with elegant utensils. Yet another group did nothing but tell Rich how wonderful he was. When these groups weren't working, which wasn't often, they enjoyed trying to top each other with stories about silly and pointless things Rich would ask them to do.

Rich and his antics provided great material for Talky Beaver, who, in addition to crack reporting, also published a regular gossip column. Every week, he riveted the island with baseless speculation about Rich's friends, relatives, and party guests. Did Rich pay off his aunt to stay quiet about some family secrets? Who stayed overnight with Rich after his garden party? Say, why isn't Rich married?

Unfortunately for Rich, because he was so rich, he also paid out a lot of cheese in taxes, which he had always felt was unfair. While this was not the first time Rich had come to complain to a Council member about this problem, it was the first time for Pol to be on the receiving end of such a complaint.

"Nice to meet you, Rich," said Pol. "What's on your mind?"

"I'd like to talk to you about the recent legislation that the Council passed to help Poor Church Mice," replied Rich is his usual snooty way. "I understand the demands of politics, but I don't think Council members gave this legislation enough thought. I'm worried that they underestimated the potential negative effects of the higher tax rate for the wealthy."

"What do you mean?" inquired Pol.

"Well," replied Rich, "it's true that I have a huge amount of cheese, but I do many good works for the community. I employ a lot of animals, and I support many worthy groups by generously donating some of my cheese. But all of the good I'm doing is at risk now because of the higher taxes I'm going to be required to pay. It's scandalous, actually. Can you believe the unfairness? I can't."

"Rich," said Pol, hardly believing what he was hearing, "I can understand your position. But I can't go before the Council and argue that the richest animal on the island needs tax relief."

"You're looking at this the wrong way," replied Rich. "I'm not asking for a handout. What I'm asking for is some assistance in exchange for the important help I provide to so many."

"What do you have in mind?" asked Pol skeptically.

"I want the Council to apply the new higher tax rates to the middle class, not just the wealthy," said Rich. "I also want the Council to create some targeted exemptions and complicated credits to offset some of these higher taxes. Of course, the Council will need to spend some cheese promoting this as a good idea since the middle class won't immediately see the wonderful benefits."

"I don't know about this," said Pol. "I was elected to keep taxes low, to ensure that taxes are spent wisely, and to keep tax cheese away from well-connected rats. No offense, but this plan fails on all counts."

"Pol," said Rich solemnly, "you know I've supported the Active Party for years. If I can't count on you and the Party to pass this plan, I don't think I'll be able to continue helping the community as I have. Unfortunately, this means that the Council is going to have to replace the assistance I provide, and that's going to be expensive."

"We certainly don't want that," responded Pol. "Let me see what I can do."

Pol worried that imploring the Council to help Rich Rat would mean the end of his political career. But his skills in delivering just the right speech had improved greatly, and once again, the Council approved another of Pol's requests.

***

"Councilmember Pol, it's a pleasure to meet you," said yet another visitor. "My name is Spotless Rat."

Spotless was a tall and skinny rat—skin, fur, and bones mostly. He thought eating was a messy affair, so he didn't do much of it.

Totally preoccupied with cleaning and neatness, Spotless spent inordinate amounts of time making sure that everything around him was, well, spotless. Members of the mental health community had taken notice, and some felt that his behavior warranted medication if not confinement in a psychiatric facility. In addition, Spotless had odd speech habits, frequently making a strange smacking sound anytime he spoke.

Spotless spent nearly every waking moment arguing for a cleaner environment, and he really disliked being challenged during such arguments. Once, in a debate about some proposed environmental rules, his opponent mumbled something about doing a cost-benefit analysis, a seemingly reasonable suggestion. Spotless shrieked and smacked so loudly in response that nervous debate judges declared the contest a draw and sent everyone home.

"Nice to meet you, Spotless," said Pol. "What can I do for you?"

"We have a problem, and I think you can help," replied Spotless. "As you know, we have a growing cleanliness crisis. Animals all over the island are generating more debris than we can handle. Some of the worst culprits are store owners. As you know, they sweep a lot of dirt and leaves out of their stores everyday, which really pile up. The resulting amount of debris is unbelievable. We have to put a stop to this."

"What do you propose?" inquired Pol.

"I want the Council to approve a rule requiring store owners to take every last bit of dirt and leaves they sweep up," said Spotless, "carefully organize it all into separate piles, and then at the end of each day take the leaves down to the pasture and the dirt down to the river. I also want the Council to impose a special tax on store owners to pay for the inspectors we want you to hire to enforce this rule."

"Won't complying with what you propose take considerable effort?" asked Pol. "A lot of these stores are pretty small and won't have the employees to do all this extra work." Pol could only imagine how angry Hedge would be if he had to comply with such a rule.

"Maybe," replied Spotless. "But it's a small price to pay to eliminate all this debris. Not only that, our proposal will generate a lot of new jobs."

"I don't know about this," worried Pol. "This is really going to hurt small store owners. In addition, I was elected to keep taxes low, to ensure that taxes are spent wisely, and to keep tax cheese away from well-connected rats. No offense, but your plan fails on all counts."

"Look," said Spotless testily, smacking between words more than usual, "we in the Clean Island movement have always worked hard to deliver votes and campaign cheese to the Active Party because its members support us. Do you really want to be known as the Active Party Council member who hates the Clean Island movement? Because that's what we'll say if anyone asks."

"I do count on your support," said Pol meekly. "Let me see what I can do."

Pol gave the conversation some thought. Spotless expressed some seemingly valid concerns, and Pol wanted to help him. But he worried about the potential impact on animals like Hedge. This kind of rule would create real hardship for them. After a few minutes, though, Pol decided that in the best interests of everyone, he should support the proposal Spotless had outlined. Besides, deep down, Pol cared about having a clean island, and he certainly didn't want voters to think otherwise.

***

The flurry of Council activity provided great material for Talky Beaver. His glowing reports on Council projects, new help for Poor Church Mice, and progress on cleaning up Freedom Island made him very popular with the Council. Talky regularly secured exclusive interviews with Council members, particularly Pol. His career advanced quickly, and he received special invitations to all the major political events.

***

About a year after Pol took office, it became clear that the Council's cheese levels were becoming dangerously low. Cheese spending had grown substantially, while tax revenue seemed to be falling. The Council met in an emergency session.

"We must raise cheese taxes," said the Esteemed Leader. "We cannot allow our cheese accounts to be depleted."

After several hours of debate, the Council passed a massive tax increase. Fortunately for Biz Rat, Rich Rat, and other well-connected rats, the tax increase legislation had loopholes that enabled them to avoid the higher taxes altogether simply by restructuring their affairs.

***

Hedge and Pol had not spoken for many months. It was true that Pol's Council activities were taking up a lot of his time, but, frankly, he had lost interest in the good government initiatives Hedge was supporting, so there was little reason to check in with Hedge. One day, however, they did manage to get together.

"Hedge, great to see you," exclaimed Pol as Hedge entered his office. "It's been way too long. I can't believe we haven't had time to see each other. How are you?"

"Not too well, actually," replied Hedge. He noticed that Pol had replaced his simple wooden desk with a much larger and fancier one. In fact, Pol's office now had a tall desk chair, fancy floors, and new windows. It was all quite luxurious.

"What's the matter? Is there something wrong with the work you're doing on the initiatives?" asked Pol, faking his interest in Hedge's efforts.

"No, nothing like that," said Hedge. "I've been having trouble with the store."

"What trouble?" asked Pol.

"It's terrible," replied Hedge. "A few months ago, they announced a new rule about store debris. You wouldn't believe the amount of work I have to do to comply. I had to hire more employees to help me."

"I'm sorry to hear this," said Pol nervously.

"What's worse, I have to pay a special tax just to support the inspectors," continued Hedge. "In addition, my other taxes have gone up, and Tax Rat's collectors now come every day. Some days, they take every last bit of cheese I have. You're on the Council, do you know why all this is happening?"

It's hard for a rat to blush visibly, what with all the fur, but Pol managed somehow.

"I, um," stammered Pol. "I know a little about this. We did have to pass some important legislation that resulted in some new rules and new taxes, but these measures were for the benefit of everyone. Frankly, though, I'm not sure whether—"

"You know about these new rules and taxes?" interrupted Hedge, standing up from his chair and gritting his teeth in anger.

"Well, just a little," lied Pol. "I can tell you that we had to do it. No choice, really."

"No choice?" exclaimed Hedge. "How could the Council approve these outrageous rules and taxes?"

"Now, Hedge, that's a little harsh," replied Pol lamely. "You're not thinking about all the wonderful benefits. Aren't you glad we're taking steps to clean up Freedom Island? Aren't you happy to see all the jobs that Biz Rat's meadow project created?"

"Biz Rat?" shouted Hedge. "Now it all makes sense! I seem to remember Biz coming to see you right after you took office. That crook! He's as corrupt as the day is long, and I'll bet he convinced you to lower his taxes to support his project. And then you passed tax increases for everyone else to compensate!"

"Hedge," said Pol calmly, "that was a one-off deal, and we did it just to ensure the success of the investment and resulting job creation." Pol's second lie in the conversation was easier than his first.

"Pol, you disappoint me," said Hedge. "You promised to lower taxes, spend taxes wisely, and stop catering to the well-connected. You've broken every one of these promises!"

"But Hedge," replied Pol. Before Pol could continue, Hedge stormed out of his office.

***

Hedge was furious. But he didn't know what to do. On his way home, he decided to stop by the river for a drink. He needed to calm down, but more importantly, he needed to do some thinking.

"Hi there. Aren't you Hedge Hedgehog?" said a stranger.

"Yes. And you are...?"

"Connector Mouse, but you can call me Conn."

"That's an interesting name," replied Hedge.

"Well, my claim to fame is knowing a lot of animals," said Conn. "Over the years, I've built up a large network of friends and acquaintances. I try to add someone to my network everyday."

"Which is why you're talking to me, I suppose," said Hedge dryly.

"Bingo," said Conn.

Conn was relatively large for a mouse, but slim and agile. His eyes glimmered when he talked, and you could always tell when he was excited or agitated, as his whiskers would twitch visibly.

No one spent more time meeting other animals and networking than Conn. Actually, networking was a natural consequence of Conn's first job in sales. Over the years, he used his network to build a successful marketing enterprise. Eventually, he launched a business teaching others how to network. His reputation meant that seats in his seminars never went unfilled.

After some brief small talk, Hedge and Conn struck up a more serious conversation.

"You seem a little gloomy," said Conn at one point. "Is there anything troubling you?"

"Well, yes," said Hedge. He began to describe his relationship with Pol and what had happened since Pol became a Council member.

"I know Politico Rat," said Conn.

"You do?" responded Hedge.

"Yes," said Conn. "I met him a few months ago at a party in his honor."

"Don't tell me, it was Biz Rat's party," sighed Hedge.

"Well, Biz Rat was there, but I saw many other movers and shakers as well," said Conn. "Do you know Biz?"

"Sort of," replied Hedge. "It's a long story. Suffice it to say that I'm sure there was some cheesy business going on at that party."

"No doubt about it," said Conn. "Unfortunately, we won't be able to count on Talky Beaver anymore to report on such things."

"What do you mean?" asked Hedge.

"He was at the party, too," replied Conn. "But all he did was laugh it up with the other guests, who praised him nearly as much as they praised Pol. By the time the evening was over, Talky had eaten so many fermented elderberries that he was too drunk to get home by himself. Funny how we didn't see that reported in the story about the party the next day."

Hedge and Conn continued their conversation well into the night. After a few more meetings, they found themselves talking almost every day. Conn would come by the store after closing, and the two of them would talk about the day's events. Inevitably, the conversation turned to politics.

One day, Conn arrived at the store with some news.

"Guess what," said Conn. "I hear that someone is challenging Pol in his first race for reelection."

"Really?" said Hedge. "Who is it?"

"Community Rat," said Conn.

"No kidding!" exclaimed Hedge. "She's terrific. I hope she wins."

"Not a chance," said Conn. "All the big names are supporting Pol. Biz Rat, Spotless Rat, Rich Rat, Fairness Rat—they're all backing Pol. There's no way he'll lose."

Conn was right. Although Community Rat had a wonderful reputation and track record, she simply couldn't overcome Pol's advantage. It seemed like Pol had campaign signs, campaign rallies, and campaign workers everywhere. In the final tally, Pol won by a landslide, with a vote margin of nearly four to one.

IV

Pol ran unopposed in his next several reelection bids. His huge victory over Community Rat discouraged subsequent political competition. In addition, the Council had secretly begun manipulating voting districts to make it harder for challengers to unseat incumbents. Within a short period, it became almost unheard of for a Council member to lose a reelection bid.

As time passed, Pol's relationships with the many rats who were trying to influence him became stronger and stronger. Every time they met with Pol, they grew bolder in what they requested of him.

"Hello, Pol," said Rich Rat, "great to see you."

"Great to see you, too," replied Pol. "Thanks for having me!"

Rich had invited Pol on an all-expense-paid trip to one of his lavish estate parties. By now, Rich had become so wealthy that the opulence of his many homes simply defied imagination. Even though he was by far the wealthiest animal on Freedom Island, he barely made the list of the top 100 taxpayers.

"This is really fabulous, Rich," shouted Pol over the noisy crowd. "You've outdone yourself!"

"Well, it wouldn't have been possible without the tax relief you secured for me," replied Rich with a wink. "The amount of cheese I've saved as a result is unbelievable. I've even used some of the cheese savings to support my charities."

"Not all of it, fortunately," replied Pol, surveying the richly catered party and returning a sly wink of his own. "So, what else can I do for you?"

"Now that you mention it..." continued Rich as he handed Pol some cheese.

He pulled Pol aside to a quieter spot and launched into a discussion about a dozen new tax breaks he felt he deserved. They were, of course, critical to the continued prosperity of Freedom Island, not to mention his own. All that was required was a little help from the Council.

Pol didn't hesitate to offer his full support. He assured Rich that he could convince the Council to approve his requests, which of course he did.

"By the way, thanks a lot for paying to have all those signs produced for my last campaign," said Pol. "I've never seen so many signs! Everywhere I looked, I saw one. It was great!"

***

Pol developed similarly good relationships with Fairness Rat, Biz Rat, and Spotless Rat.

"Fairness, my radical friend, how are you?" asked Pol. "That was a fantastic speech."

Fairness had just spoken at a rally for the benefit of Poor Church Mice, which Pol had supported using a special Council fund. She had really whipped up the audience with her speech, in which she urged everyone to petition the Council for yet more cheese for the poor.

"Thanks, Pol. I have such fun doing this," replied Fairness, her bracelets and necklaces clanking away.

"Tell me, Fairness," inquired Pol, "where do you find the time to write all these speeches and organize these events? This is the tenth rally you've had this month."

"Well, thanks to generous cheese subsidies from the Council, I've been able to hire an enormous staff," answered Fairness. "I have four speechwriters, three event planners, five promotion assistants, and a personal secretary. I'm much more effective now at talking about helping Poor Church Mice than I was before, thanks to you. Here, have some cheese!"

"That's great to hear," said Pol. "What else can I do for you?"
"Now that you mention it...," replied Fairness.

***

"Biz!" shouted Pol across the room. He had spotted his good friend at yet another lavish party for Council members.

"Pol! Talk to me, baby!" replied Biz.

"It's all about you, Biz!" said Pol. "By the way, I've been meaning to ask you about your meadow project, which the Council supported with tax breaks a while back. How's the project going?"

"To be honest, I don't know how it could have turned out better," replied Biz. "I continue to earn more cheese on that project than on any other. I sure appreciate all the help you've given me. That provision you slipped into Council legislation last year to make my tax breaks permanent means that I'll make cheese on my meadow project forever! You can absolutely count on my support in your future campaigns. Here, have some cheese!"

"That's great to hear," said Pol. "What else can I do for you?"

"Now that you mention it...," replied Biz.

***

"Spotless, you old rat, how are you?" exclaimed Pol. The latest Clean Island conference had just wrapped up, and Pol had been a keynote speaker. This was Pol's first opportunity to catch up with Spotless since the start of the conference.

"I'm great, Pol!" replied Spotless.

"Say," said Pol, "are things as good in the Clean Island movement as they seem?"

"Couldn't be better," answered Spotless with a few smacks. "Thanks to you, we now have nearly 500 Clean Island rules on the books."

Since Pol had taken office, more than half of the small stores on Freedom Island had closed down, largely because of the debris rules and special debris taxes, which had been raised a dozen times since they were initially enacted.

"I guess you heard the latest statistic, which is that large numbers of stores have closed because of the debris rules and taxes," said Pol.

"Those small stores couldn't comply sufficiently, so it's better that they're gone," replied Spotless. "The store owners were just exploiting our environment anyway. Maybe now they'll find some honest work that will help keep Freedom Island clean instead of doing damage. Here, have some cheese!"

"You're absolutely right," said Pol. "What else can I do for you?"
"Now that you mention it...," replied Spotless.

***

"Not long ago," the Esteemed Leader announced to an emergency session of the Council, "I came to you to address a cheese crisis. You responded with a healthy and appropriate increase in the cheese tax. Now, however, we have another crisis. We're nearly out of cheese again. We may need to raise taxes once more."

"Sir," inquired Pol, "why don't we just borrow some cheese? A few loans will get us through the crisis. That way, we won't have to raise taxes. I'm sure we'll be able to repay the cheese we borrow once the Freedom Island economy improves."

"Pol," exclaimed the Esteemed Leader, "that's a brilliant idea!" It passed the Council overwhelmingly.

***

"Hi, Hedge," said Conn as he walked into the store one day. "Have you seen today's paper?"

"I haven't," replied Hedge. "Anything interesting?"

"Talky Beaver is now the Executive Editor," said Conn. "He was appointed yesterday."

"Time to cancel our subscriptions," said Hedge. "Talky has gotten too close to the Council. I think he's lost his objectivity."

"I agree," said Conn.

"It's too bad, really," continued Hedge. "Talky used to be a crack reporter who could get to the bottom of any corruption story. Now he's just a mouthpiece for Pol and other members of the Active Party. If all you read were his stories, you'd never think there was a single thing wrong with what the Active Party does."

"Fortunately," interrupted Conn as he pulled out some additional papers, "I've found some alternative news sources. Take a look at these headlines from a new competing paper that launched last month."

"Massive Waste and Fraud Uncovered in Council-Funded Meadow Project"

"Tons of Cheese Spent Helping Poor Church Mice—Poverty Level Unchanged"

"Tax Avoidance by the Wealthy Soars"

"Council Budget Deficit Reaches Record Levels—No End in Sight"

"Can you believe this?" thundered Hedge as he banged his paws on the counter. "If this keeps up, they'll bankrupt Freedom Island!"

"Should we get the group together tonight to talk about it?" asked Conn.

"Absolutely," said Hedge. "I've got some new ideas we simply must discuss."

About a year ago, soon after Pol's most recent election victory, Hedge, Conn, and several friends decided to form a group called "Animals for Honest Government." Hedge clearly had the most passion about the group's work, and he had emerged as its leader.

Initially, the group's discussions focused on a broad set of issues related to honesty in government. Lately, however, the focus was more on problems with the Council. The debates were contentious, as no one could agree on what the real problems were, let alone what solutions might work.

Conn succeeded in contacting the group about meeting that night, and nearly everyone said they could attend. Later that day, as Hedge and Conn walked over to the local lodge hall to prepare for the meeting, they continued talking.

"You know," said Conn, "those headlines were incredible. Until I saw them, I had no idea that the problems being caused by the Council were so severe."

"It's probably even worse than what's reported," replied Hedge.

That night, the group argued for hours. In the end, with encouragement from Hedge and Conn, they decided that the best way forward was to change party allegiances. Although everyone in the group had been longtime members of the Active Party, they decided it was time to switch and support candidates from the Limited Party.

It was an interesting course of action. The Limited Party had long been a minority player on the Council. But Hedge and Conn sensed growing public unhappiness with the Active Party and felt that Animals for Honest Government could help drive needed change. They believed that if they could help the Limited Party achieve a majority on the Council, things would improve dramatically.

In the weeks following this decision, Hedge and Conn met with several Limited Party leaders. They convinced them that their party needed to appeal to voters disgusted with how the Council had deteriorated over the years. Party leaders agreed. They soon devised a comprehensive "Contract with Freedom Island," wherein they vowed that their candidates would work to clean up the Council.

Over that next year, Hedge, Conn, and the rest of Animals for Honest Government worked tirelessly to identify and support Limited Party candidates. They fielded a particularly strong candidate to try to unseat Pol. Reform Rat, who was a longtime friend of Conn's, had superb credentials. Everyone was convinced that if anyone could clean up government, it was Reform Rat.

Reform was an even stronger proponent of better government than Hedge. Up until a few years ago, Reform was an ordinary, middle-aged rat who worked in a cheese-making shop. He had earned his name and reputation by constantly suggesting ways to reform the cheese-making process. One day, he discovered that large quantities of cheese were disappearing from the shop's storage area. When he brought it to the attention of management, he got nowhere. In fact, his manager turned the tables on him by falsely claiming that his performance had deteriorated and eventually fired him. Soon after his termination, some sympathetic insiders still working at the shop told Reform that management, along with several Council members, had orchestrated a cheese thieving scheme for their own benefit.

Furious and determined to fight back, Reform turned to Talky Beaver for help. He was sure that with Talky on his side, he could expose the corruption and restore his reputation, perhaps even his job. But by then, Talky himself had become corrupted. Instead of faithfully reporting what should have been an explosive story, Talky published a ridiculous puff piece that basically whitewashed the entire affair—something to the effect that the missing cheese had too many holes and had simply been thrown out, and even if that weren't exactly true, the cheese shop managers and their Council friends were in fact wonderful rats with nice families, interesting hobbies, blah, blah, blah.

Reform was outraged. Over the next year, he worked to identify other animals who were similarly upset about Council corruption and mismanagement. By the time Hedge approached him about running for a seat on the Council, he had become a fairly well-known political activist. Though a little reluctant at first, Reform finally agreed to become a Council candidate.

As Election Day approached, prospects for Limited Party candidates seemed promising, despite the voting group manipulation that the Active Party had engaged in to protect its majority status. When returns finally came in, it became clear that everyone's efforts had paid off. The Limited Party candidates won an outright majority on the Council for the first time. After all the years of frustration, Hedge and Conn believed that the Council would finally be restored to its original integrity and noble purpose.

The sweetest victory of all, of course, was the defeat of Pol. Reform Rat had beaten him by ten points at the polls. On Election Night, after word came in that Pol had conceded, Reform delivered an exhilarating victory speech.

"Friends," Reform began, "we have won a great victory. Our many years in the political wilderness have come to an end. We finally have a chance to implement the real reform we have all sought for so long. As your newly elected Council member, I promise to do all I can to keep taxes low, ensure that taxes are spent wisely, and end the practice of granting special privileges to well-connected rats."

The crowd jumped to its feet, shouting and applauding as Reform spoke.

"Reform Rat—Better Government! Reform Rat—Better Government!"

***

The Limited Party-dominated Council got off to a promising start. Initially, the rules they enacted to implement real reform seemed spot on. Hedge and Conn couldn't believe how well everything was turning out. Hedge remarked how things were beginning to feel 'normal' again.

Unfortunately, their early satisfaction soon began to fade.

At first, the problems were subtle. Despite his campaign promises, Reform Rat somehow ended up supporting Council measures that neglected to "keep taxes low." In addition, for some reason, scandals and evidence of corruption in Council work began to reappear. Hedge and Conn couldn't figure out why problems like this were resurfacing, especially since Reform had pledged to eliminate them.

As time passed, waste, corruption, and mismanagement grew more serious, exceeding even the worst of the Active Party years. Hedge and Conn felt as if the old Council had returned. Their suspicions were confirmed one day when they saw Biz, Fairness, Rich, and Spotless all leaving Reform's office, arm in arm. The four old rats were laughing as they had never laughed before.

"I can't believe this," muttered Conn. "We worked so hard to get a Limited Party majority on the Council, and look where we are. Nowhere."

"That's not our worst problem," replied Hedge.

"What do you mean?" asked Conn.

"Here, take a look," said Hedge. He handed Conn a notice he had received just that day.

"Eviction?" said Conn. "They can't evict you. You own this store."

"That's what I thought," replied Hedge. "According to this, the Council has the right take someone's property in exchange for minimal compensation of its choosing. Apparently, they want to tear down my store because they need the land."

"For what?" asked Conn.

"Biz and Rich have hired a large number of rats to work on influencing the Council," replied Hedge. "They need space for them. I have thirty days to close up everything."

V

The eviction notice came as a real blow to Hedge. For the first time in his life, he felt completely powerless.

"I'm going for a walk," said Hedge. "Would you mind the store for a while?"

"Sure," said Conn.

Hedge walked out slowly. Like he had done many times in the past, he went down to the river for a drink. The sound of the water seemed to have a calming effect on him. As he listened, he began to feel better.

"Hedge?" asked someone from behind. Hedge turned and saw an old rat standing in front of him. It was Preacher Rat, a family friend Hedge had not seen since childhood.

"Preacher!" exclaimed Hedge, rising to his feet. "I can't believe it! How are you? What are you doing here?"

"Well, let's just say that you have a very good friend in Conn," replied Preacher. "He contacted me after you left the store and told me I might find you here."

"I can't tell you how wonderful it is to see you," said Hedge. They began to talk about old times, and about Hedge's elderly parents, who still lived on the other side of town in the same place where Hedge grew up.

"Conn tells me that you're having some trouble, my son," said Preacher at one point. "What's wrong? Can I help you?"

"I don't know, Preacher," replied Hedge as he sat back down dejectedly. He began to describe what had been going on politically. He recounted how he had supported Politico Rat, then Reform Rat, and how it had all gone wrong.

"You know, maybe I'm overreacting," continued Hedge. "I mean, look around. We have the most prosperous animal society ever conceived. We have a fantastic economy. We have a wonderful standard of living. True, there are clearly some problems with the Council, its morals, and its finances. But given how good everything else seems, why should I care? Maybe everything really is OK."

Preacher sat down and remained silent.

"After all," Hedge continued, "we're still a lot better off than animals ever were on Animal Farm. That place was miserable, and it was ruled by an awful dictator. We have no such problems here. Like our anthem says, tyranny is dead! Long live Freedom Island!"

Hedge and Preacher sat there quietly for a few moments. After a while, Preacher finally spoke.

"Hedge," said Preacher, "how would you characterize the evil that plagued Animal Farm?"

"Characterize it?" said Hedge. "Well, I guess I would say that it had two aspects. First, it grew almost unnoticed over a long period. Tyranny emerged on Animal Farm, but very slowly, as did all the problems associated with it, like hunger, misery, and exploitation. The animals might have realized what was going on earlier, but Napoleon and the other pigs deceived them on a regular basis and lied anytime someone raised questions. The second aspect was that once it became clear that Animal Farm had succumbed to a terrible tyranny, the animals couldn't do anything about it. It was too late."

Hedge paused for a moment.

"Thank goodness we've never succumbed to such evil," he continued with a sigh of relief. "Even after receiving today's eviction notice, I still feel we're a long way from the tyranny of Animal Farm. We live in an open society. We have problems, but they don't seem out of control. Even more importantly, our Freedom Rules haven't been corrupted. As I said, maybe I'm overreacting. Maybe things really are OK."

"The thing you have to remember about evil," interrupted Preacher, "is that it comes in many forms. Sometimes it's obvious, sometimes it's not so obvious. Sometimes it's easy to identify and correct, sometimes not. Just because everything seems fine on the surface doesn't mean there's no evil lurking below the surface."

"I hadn't thought about it that way," said Hedge.

"There's something else you should know," continued Preacher. "Animals are pretty bad at dealing with more subtle, hard-to-spot forms of evil

"What do you mean?" asked Hedge.

"They're blind to it," replied Preacher. "If the evil is slow-moving and makes its effects felt only over a long period of time, animals don't notice. They simply allow it to grow. When a few individuals do sense something's wrong, they're loudly dismissed by others who don't. As a result, no action is taken. That's why subtle forms of evil are so dangerous. They often grow into more obvious and destructive forms of evil, and by then it's usually too late to do anything about them. That's what I believe happened on Animal Farm."

Hedge sat silently for a moment.

"Hedge," continued Preacher, "in my opinion, I think you've stumbled upon a great evil that's slowly infecting *our* society. You think you might be overreacting, but you're not. You're just able to see the evil that threatens us in a way that others can't. Bear in mind, too, that this evil is in a different form than the one that infected Animal Farm. If it continues to grow unchecked, though, the result will eventually be the same. We will succumb to an awfully tyranny."

Preacher put his paws on Hedge's shoulders and looked him in the eye.

"The question is," he said firmly, "are you going to help the animals of Freedom Island see this evil and do something about it? Or are you going to join them in ignorance by continuing to claim that tyranny is dead? It's up to you."

Hedge pondered Preacher's words. Soon, a fiery sparkle came to his eyes.

"Preacher, thank you," said Hedge boldly as he stood.

"Well, I hope I've been helpful in some way, Hedge," said Preacher.

"More than you know," replied Hedge.

With that, Hedge made his way back to the store. He hadn't moved his legs that quickly in a long time.

VI

A bell on the front door clanged loudly as Hedge burst into his store. He'd been gone only a few hours.

"Hedge!" said Conn, startled.

"Conn, thanks for sending Preacher to see me," said Hedge quickly as he walked up to the counter. "He was very helpful."

"No problem," replied Conn. "What did he tell you?"

"A lot of things," replied Hedge, "but the main thing he told me was that I shouldn't give up my fight to restore good government on Freedom Island."

"So what do we do next?" asked Conn.

"It's time to reconvene Animals for Honest Government," replied Hedge. "Let's see if we can get the gang together tonight."

Over the years, Animals for Honest Government had grown considerably, both in size and diversity. The membership ranks included rabbits, hens, cats, mice, squirrels, porcupines, and others. Political diversity abounded as well, as there seemed to be equal numbers of Active Party and Limited Party supporters. For all its diversity, the group did find itself united on at least one point: the need to restore integrity and efficiency in government.

Thanks to Conn's efforts, word about that night's meeting spread quickly. Most members showed up, leaving hardly any open seats in the lodge hall. Noisy conversations filled the air, as members tried to catch up with each other, often resurrecting unfinished debates from prior sessions. Soon, Hedge called the meeting to order.

"Friends, we've been meeting for a long time," said Hedge. "We've worked on problems together. We've worked on campaigns together. We've elected so-called reform candidates together. And yet, we've made little if any progress in restoring integrity and efficiency to our government."

Everyone murmured in agreement.

"We need to reenergize our efforts and develop some fresh thinking," Hedge continued. "I have some ideas, but do any of you?"

"Well, I don't know what the rest of you think," offered one animal, "but I believe we need to improve oversight of public works projects. What about supporting the formation of a special oversight commission?"

"That's not a bad idea," interrupted another animal, "but the commission should oversee more than public works. What about Council departments as well?"

"You're both right," said a third animal, "but let's not forget what's really important. We must petition the Council to rethink its approach to environmental rules. We're not doing enough to help clean up Freedom Island."

"More environmental rules?" exclaimed yet another animal. "Are you kidding? The rules we have now are almost beyond counting."

"Forget about cleaning up the island," interrupted another animal. "What about Poor Church Mice? They're starving while the Council does nothing!"

"Yes, but..." started another animal.

"Hold on, everyone!" shouted Hedge above the fray. Hedge possessed a commanding voice, and he could get a crowd's attention when necessary.

"These are good debates," he continued, "but they're the same debates we always have. And the reason we keep having these debates is because no matter what we or anyone else does, none of the problems underlying the debates ever gets resolved. Haven't you ever wondered about this?"

Hedge paused to survey the room, which had grown quiet.

"Perhaps the reason we can't make any progress," he went on, "is because we're not seeing what the real problem is. I have a new theory about this that I'd like to share with you tonight. In my view, the challenge we face can be distilled into a single statement."

Hedge pulled out a poster and wrote out the following:

The Rats are in the Cheese

"The rats are in the cheese?" said one animal. "What does that mean?"

"It means that our entire political existence is governed and controlled by rats in their unending quest to get cheese," said Hedge confidently.

"Hedge, why don't you give them some examples of what you mean," said Conn.

"Good idea, Conn," said Hedge. "Here goes. As most of you know, I've owned and operated a small store for many years. At first, I paid only one tax. The last time Tax Rat's collectors stopped by, however, I had to pay fourteen different taxes and fees. It took two hours for them just to explain it all to me. By the time they were done, it took all the cheese I had to pay the resulting tax bill."

"That's terrible!" said one animal.

"It gets worse," Hedge continued. "The next day, one of Tax Rat's collectors came by my home. She announced cheerily that in addition to store taxes, I also owed personal taxes. She then proceeded to describe sixteen different taxes, fees, assessments, and levies. It was overwhelming. She ended up taking nearly half of my personal cheese in taxes. On top of all this, the Council has decided that it needs the land where my store is located to make room for rats whose full-time job will be to influence Council decision-making. I've paid all these taxes for years, and now they're taking away my store!"

Cries of "outrageous," "unbelievable," and "that doesn't seem fair" rang throughout the hall.

"That's my story about how the rats are in the cheese," said Hedge. "What about some of you?"

One animal, a large woodchuck, threw his paw up first. "Remember that report about Farmer Rat?" he asked. "He wasn't making enough money farming, so he went to the Council to ask for help. And do you know what they did? They passed a law that provides free cheese to him and the other farmers for not farming. In other words, they get cheese for doing nothing!"

Another animal, a small cat with a high-pitched voice, raised her paw next. "I'll go you one better. Did everyone hear about Research Rat? The Council just approved massive cheese funding for a research project he proposed. For the next two years, Research Rat and his large, highly paid team will conduct a study to find out why there's water in the river. Can you believe it?"

"I have another story," interrupted a talkative goat. "I was down by the pasture the other day, and someone told me some news about Nervous Rat. You all know him; he's that jumpy rat you can hardly talk to because he's so tense and anxious. Well, Lawyer Rat petitioned the Council, claiming that Nervous has a 'disabling condition.' So the Council voted to give Nervous free cheese for life. They also paid Lawyer a big pile of cheese for taking it upon himself to bring the matter to the Council's attention."

A hen raised her wing. "And did everyone hear about all the cheese being spent on cultural activities?" she said. "I heard yesterday that the Council approved free cheese for Artist Rat, Opera Rat, and Sculpture Rat. Apparently, animals aren't paying them enough cheese to see or hear their works. Frankly, I can't blame them. Have any of you sat through one of Opera Rat's marathon concerts? It's nothing short of torture."

"Does anyone care to guess where the Council is getting the cheese to pay for all this?" asked an old rooster.

"From Hedge?" someone joked.

"Not entirely!" said the rooster, laughing. "Last week, I had lunch with Pension Rat, who runs the Freedom Island pension trust set up by the Council."

"What does the pension trust have to do with spending cheese?" asked a gopher. "I thought the trust was set up to store cheese to support old animals in their retirement."

"That's what I thought, too," said the rooster. "But Pension told me that the cheese animals have been paying into the trust has already been spent by the Council."

"So there's no extra cheese to help pay future benefits?" asked the gopher.

"No, there isn't," said the rooster. "Like I said, it's all gone."

"So how will future benefits be paid?" asked the gopher, clearly surprised.

"Higher taxes," replied the rooster. "In fact, given how generously the Council has increased benefits over the years, taxes are going to have to get a lot higher to pay every benefit that has been promised."

"There's even more to this story!" interjected Conn, interrupting the rooster. "All the cheese taxes and all the cheese that the Council is appropriating from the pension trust are not enough to cover all the cheese spending. To make up the shortfall, they've started borrowing cheese. Go down by the river after dark on any night and you'll see big rafts loaded with cheese being docked at the riverbank. Other animal communities upriver are working overtime to produce cheese so they can lend it to the Council. I hope I'm not around when these loans come due."

Conn's remarks upset the group considerably. For the next several moments, members shouted back and forth at each other. It was clear that none of them realized how bad things had gotten.

"OK, everyone," said Hedge as he tried to calm the group down. "I think the point has been made. What's disturbing to me is that a lot of these shenanigans have taken place without everyone's full knowledge."

"Exactly," added Conn. "Publicly, Council members offer lofty and important reasons for each decision they make, but behind the scenes they load every law they pass with cheese tax giveaways and cheese spending that a majority of animals would find outrageous. The problem is that most animals never really hear about the details."

"In my view," continued Hedge, "this is all because the rats are in the cheese. Somehow, every one of the Council's schemes results in large slices of cheese going to well-connected rats. Slowly but surely, our society is being ruined as a result. Our anthem proudly proclaims that 'tyranny is dead,' but is it coming back to life in a new form? I'm worried that it is."

"Hedge," said a voice near the front of the room. It was Nutsy Squirrel, a quick little rodent with a razor-sharp mind. Crazy antics in his youth had earned him his nickname, which had stuck with him over the years.

"You're wrong about all this," he continued. "It's true that the rats are in the cheese, but they always have been to some extent. The problems everyone has described tonight have been going on for years, even since the founding of Freedom Island. But take a look around. We live in a largely free and very prosperous society, the envy of animal societies everywhere. This is not Animal Farm. There is no dictatorship. No one is distorting our Freedom Rules like they did with the old commandments on Animal Farm. It seems to me that we've done pretty well for ourselves despite the problems we've been discussing. In other words, you're overreacting. Everything is fine. Relax."

"Good points, Nutsy," said Hedge as the eyes of the group turned back to him. "But not good enough. You're right that the rats have been in the cheese for a long time. What's different now, though, is that they're becoming a lot more aggressive, both in terms of how much cheese they're getting, and how they're keeping the public from really understanding what they're doing."

Hedge turned back to the audience.

"Let me use an analogy to describe what I'm thinking," he continued. "Years ago, having rats in the cheese was like having fleas, annoying but not life-threatening. Today, it's like having a slow-growing but painless cancer. You can't see or feel it, but one day soon it will kill you. Based on the stories we've all told each other tonight, I think it's clear that we're facing a kind of painless but ultimately lethal cancer in our society. It's not too late to do something about it if we take action now."

"I'm not buying it, Hedge," said Nutsy. "Again, you're overreacting. This is not Animal Farm. Tyranny is still dead."

"No it's not," replied Hedge sharply. "And I can prove it to you."

"How?" asked Nutsy.

"Come with me over to the town square," said Hedge. "I'll show you."

The group sat silently for a moment, not knowing what to do.

"Let's go, everyone!" shouted Hedge. "Besides, it's getting stuffy in here."

Reluctantly, everyone rose to their feet and headed out the door. Conn led the way. Hedge and Nutsy continued to argue as they strolled toward the town square.

After a short walk, the group arrived at the square. Everyone gathered around the Freedom Rules Monument. Hedge stood on a nearby rock to address the group.

"The moon is pretty bright tonight," said Hedge. "Can everyone see the Freedom Rules?" Everyone murmured that they could, so he continued.

"These words describe our most basic rights," said Hedge pointing to the Freedom Rules. "But what do you notice about them? One thing I notice is that they haven't changed. They're the same words that our founders originally chose."

"Precisely," interrupted Nutsy. "As I said earlier, our Freedom Rules remain intact. No one has compromised or twisted what the founders wrote like they did on Animal Farm."

"Are you sure about that?" asked Hedge. "I'm not. Let me show you."

Hedge stepped down from the rock and walked over to the monument. "Look at this first rule," said Hedge as he pointed to the monument. *"All animals are equal before the law."*

Pausing for a moment, he then turned to Nutsy.

"The words haven't changed, but why is it that Rich Rat gets tax breaks and we don't?" Hedge continued. "Why does Research Rat get a huge cheese grant for some pointless study and we don't? Why do Farmer Rat and Nervous Rat get cheese subsidies for life and we don't? Even though it's not apparent in writing, the wording change we were warned about in the Animal Farm story has returned. All animals are equal, but some are more equal than others."

"Let's look at another rule," Hedge went on. *"The Council shall have the ability to levy reasonable taxes.* Does anyone believe that the taxes we now pay are reasonable? Does anyone think that the complexity of fourteen store taxes and sixteen personal taxes is reasonable? Does anyone consider daily visits from Tax Rat or his minions reasonable?"

Hedge stopped for a moment, then turned back to the monument.

"How about one more," he continued. *"Animals shall be governed by a Council elected every two years by majority vote.* Yes, it's true that we all get to vote every two years. But how many of you feel that your vote counts? Did anyone here get to vote on the meadow project tax benefits for Biz Rat? How about the tax breaks for Rich Rat? Did you vote on that one? When you did vote to put the Limited Party in the majority, did it matter? What changed? The fact is, even though you get to vote in the Council races, you don't really get to vote on what matters."

Hedge walked back to the rock and stepped up so he could see everyone again. "Friends," he continued, "our Freedom Rules look the same but in fact have changed significantly over time. Unfortunately, they changed so gradually that we didn't even see it happen. The result is that too many rats are in too much cheese. And we need to do something about it before real tyranny returns to haunt us again."

"Let's go back to the lodge to continue the conversation," suggested Conn. "It's getting a little chilly."

The group began walking back to the lodge. No one said a word. Once back inside, Nutsy rose to speak first.

"All right, Hedge, I'm beginning to see your point," said Nutsy after taking a deep breath. "I now agree with you that having rats in the cheese to the degree we have today is a difficult and insidious problem, and one that we need to tackle head-on. You've done a great job at helping to explain why."

The group broke into applause, with even a few cheers and whistles. Conn walked over to the poster that Hedge had written out earlier.

"Let me see if I can summarize the points we've made tonight," said Conn. "Can I get your reaction as I write each one?" He began scribbling just beneath the words 'The Rats are in the Cheese.'

1. **Council actions promote inequality before the law**
   "Right!" the group shouted in unison.
2. **Our complex taxes cheat average animals.**
   "Right again!" they shouted.
3. **We do vote for the Council, but the Council takes many actions that a majority of us would never support**
   "Right once more!" they shouted, even louder this time.

"I think we're all in agreement with what's been discussed tonight," said Nutsy. "What do we do next?"

"We have to figure out how to stop the rats from getting in the cheese," Hedge replied. "If we can do this, we'll be able to solve many other problems. Even better, some might just go away by themselves."

"But how?" asked the old rooster. "What should we do to reshape the Freedom Rules or reform the Council to eliminate these problems?"

"This is where I'm a little short on ideas," Hedge admitted. "I think we're going to need help on this. We need to consult with someone who has more experience in the workings of our government, someone who has the knowledge, but who also can see and appreciate the problem we're trying to solve."

"I think I know someone who can help us," said Conn, who as usual was at the ready with some kind of connection or acquaintance. "Have any of you met Wonk Rat before?"

Wonk was a retired professor who had been researching and teaching politics for years. He was also a rat and thus had an appreciation for rat thinking.

"Even though he's a rat," continued Conn, "he's definitely worth meeting. If anyone understands politics, the Council, and how rats get in the cheese, it's Wonk."

"Well, now that I've been retired by the Council from my store, I've got plenty of time on my hands," said Hedge. "Conn, why don't we pay a visit to your friend, Wonk?"

"He's on the far north end of the island, so it will take some time to get there," replied Conn. "Let's head out in the morning."

"Terrific!" said Hedge. "I'll pack my things tonight!" He then turned to the group. Raising his voice once more, he said, "Thank you all for coming! We'll report back as soon as we've interviewed Wonk!"

VII

T he meeting last night was amazing," said Conn as he and Hedge began their journey. "Everyone thought your insights were terrific."

"Thanks," replied Hedge. "But I think we could benefit from an even better understanding of how the rats get in the cheese, and why. I wish we could learn more before we see Professor Wonk."

"Maybe we can," said Conn. "Let's take a short detour to meet a friend of mine, Phat Mouse."

"Phat Mouse?" said Hedge.

"Phat should have been born a rat," continued Conn. "He operates all over Freedom Island, mostly on shady business deals. Oddly enough, though, he's a brutally honest mouse. He thinks he should try to separate animals from as much of their cheese as possible, and has become fairly skilled at doing so. I've known him for a while and even helped him avoid jail once, so he owes me a favor."

"When we started exploring rats and their cheese connection, I figured we might run into some unsavory characters," said Hedge. "Let's go talk to him."

Hedge and Conn arrived at Phat's office the following day.

"Conn, I've figured out yet another way to help animals part with their cheese!" said Phat enthusiastically as Hedge and Conn stepped into his office. "Your connections would be a big help. How about coming in for a piece of the action?"

Phat's cronies never seemed to leave his side. That day, two of the more suspicious-looking ones happened to be in his office. Hedge didn't seem to mind, but Conn felt a little uneasy. He knew Phat all too well.

"Forget about it, Phat," said Conn, trying to come across confidently. "You've mistaken me for one of your crooked friends."

They quickly got down to business. Hedge summed up what he and Conn had been thinking about. Phat listened intently.

"It sounds like you're pretty well-informed about rats," said Phat.

"Is there anything else we should know?" asked Hedge.

"Well, there is one thing I haven't heard you talk about," replied Phat. "And it's a pretty important concept for any rat involved in cheese thieving. But just remember that you didn't hear it from me, and don't plan on competing with me in the cheese business. It might affect your health."

"Don't worry," said Hedge. "Our mission has nothing to do with you. We're just trying to develop some public policy ideas. What else do we need to know about?"

"OAC," replied Phat.

"OAC?" asked Conn.

"Other Animals' Cheese," said Phat. "Let me see if I can explain." Phat stood up.

"Cheese is hard to steal directly from the animals who earned it," explained Phat as one of his underlings served up a big plate of cheese. "They worked hard for it, and they keep an eye on it. That's why so many small time rat thieves wind up in jail. Instead, it's much better to target cheese that has been accumulated away from the animals who earned it."

"What do you mean by that?" said Hedge.

"In a rich society like ours, cheese is accumulated everywhere on behalf of individual animals," replied Phat. "Banks, retirement funds, union treasuries, you name it. But the biggest accumulation of all is Council cheese, which the Council collects through taxation and then spends on various programs. The mere thought of all that cheese available for the taking sends my pulse racing."

"I hadn't thought about that before," said Hedge, "but you're right. Council cheese is a prime target for rats."

"Absolutely," said Phat. "In fact, I've helped run at least a hundred schemes over the years to help rats get their paws on Council cheese. And guess what? Every scheme was legal."

"For example?" said Hedge.

"Three years ago," replied Phat, "I helped convince the Council to guarantee some risky cheese loans to a bunch of cats who had fallen on hard times. I got several of my lawyer and banker friends involved to help set up the deal, and we all got to take a big cut of the loan proceeds as a fee for our services. Frankly, we hardly did any work."

Phat began to chuckle as he continued.

"Last year," he said grinning, "those stupid cats, who by then had squandered all of the cheese, defaulted on the loan. The Council stepped in to make good on its guarantee and paid back my banker friend directly. But best of all, my friends and I collected more fees for helping to set up the payback transaction. Ultimately, of course, the taxpayers paid the bill for all that nonsense. It was great."

"That's outrageous," said Conn. "All you do is help others steal cheese and take unfair advantage of our government."

"Don't be so judgmental," snapped Phat. "This kind of corruption goes on all the time. Rich or poor, connected or not, the vast majority of animals at one time or another have taken advantage of other animals' cheese. It's in their nature."

"I guess your point is that even the most honest animal can act like a rat sometimes," said Conn.

"That's right," said Phat. "And this tendency to act like a rat is particularly strong when other animals' cheese is involved."

"I think I've heard enough," said Hedge as he stood to leave.

"Me, too," said Conn. "Phat, you lead an interesting life. Too bad you can't focus your talents in a more positive way."

"You're too straight-laced, Conn," said Phat, laughing. "I wish you'd reconsider and come help me with my latest scheme. I'll make you rich!"

"I'd just slow you down," replied Conn, rolling his eyes.

"Come on, Conn," said Phat. "Look inside your heart. There's a little rat in there somewhere!"

***

Hedge and Conn continued their journey, lost in thought about what they had learned from Phat.

"Phat made some good points," said Conn.

"I agree," said Hedge. "Two things stand out in my mind. First, rats get in the cheese much more easily when the cheese has been separated from those who directly earned it."

"OAC," said Conn. "Other Animals' Cheese."

"Right," said Hedge. "And second, trying to get in the cheese is in the nature of every animal. The tendency is worse in some animals, particularly rats, but in general, all animals are like this. They can't help it."

"There is a little rat in all of us," added Conn.

After a few more days of traveling, Hedge and Conn arrived at Wonk's place. Hedge had never been to this part of the island.

"Hello, Hedge, I'm glad to meet you," said Wonk, after a brief introduction by Conn. Wonk had trouble walking and used a cane, but his mind was still plenty sharp.

"Professor Wonk, it's a privilege to make your acquaintance," replied Hedge. "I've heard a lot about you from Conn. During our journey here, he filled me in on all that you've accomplished."

"I hope some of what Conn said was good!" said the professor, laughing.

"Actually, all of it was good, which is why I'm so glad to have a chance to visit with you," said Hedge.

"Come on in," said Wonk as he gestured Hedge and Conn to step inside.

Everything about Wonk was professorial. He looked, talked and gestured like a professor. His place, filled with books, looked like a professor's classroom. The table in the middle of the main room provided a perfect spot to meet, except for the stacks of books and papers piled high.

"Sorry about the mess," said Wonk ashamedly as he cleared some space. "So, what would you like to talk about? What brings you to my ivory tower?"

"Well," said Hedge as he sat down at the table, "Conn and I are members of a political group called Animals for Honest Government. We've been working for years to promote integrity and efficiency in government. Some of our efforts have included working with individual Council members, supporting measures to promote transparency and honesty, and even campaigning to replace Council members that we believed were harming the Council. In fact, we played a leading role in the effort that led to the election of a Limited Party majority on the Council a while back."

"A lot of good that did," said Wonk sarcastically.

"We were disappointed, too," said Conn.

"Since then," continued Hedge, "we've gone back to the drawing board to reconsider what we're doing. We've determined that underlying all of the integrity and efficiency issues we face is a single problem. The rats are in the cheese."

"The rats are in the cheese?" said Wonk. "What do you mean by this?"

To answer the professor's question, Hedge and Conn rehashed their debate with Nutsy Squirrel and the rest of Animals for Honest Government.

"Here's a summary of the points we developed," said Conn as he produced the poster he and Hedge had written out.

The Rats are in the Cheese
1. **Council actions promote inequality before the law**
2. **Our complex taxes cheat average animals**
3. **We do vote for the Council, but the Council takes many actions that a majority of us would never support**

Wonk took the poster and studied it carefully.

"Professor," said Hedge, "I think our overall understanding of the problem is right, but we're having a little trouble trying to figure out what to do next."

"This is all very interesting, Hedge," said Wonk. "I'd like to see if I can help. Let me suggest that we start by analyzing the key players and what motivates them."

"Sounds great, professor," said Conn.

Wonk stood up and began to pace as he started to lecture, easily reprising his old role of classroom professor. Conveniently, he happened to have a large chalkboard, which some of his students gave to him as a gift when he retired. Wonk picked up some chalk and began writing as he talked.

"To begin with," said Wonk, "you have to keep in mind that the Council takes in and spends a vast amount of cheese. Because it's such a large amount, the taxpayers who supply the cheese and the recipients who receive the cheese all have strong incentives to shape cheese taxing and spending to their advantage. After all, everyone wants more cheese. Make sense?"

Hedge and Conn nodded in agreement.

"Because of these incentives, rats will go to great lengths to influence Council decision-making in favor of their own special interests," continued the professor. "With so much cheese at stake, it's foolish not to!"

"I hadn't thought about that," said Conn as he scratched his head. "I guess I see your point."

"Hold on, I'm just getting started," said Wonk. "Obviously, Council members have their own views and opinions. If they didn't, they wouldn't have been inspired to run for office in the first place. But once they're in office, much of what they legislate ends up being shaped in large part by what I call special interest rats."

"Why does a Council member listen to these special interest rats, especially if what they're asking for is contrary to what the Council member really believes?" asked Hedge.

"If a rat gets what he wants, he can reward the member by supplying cheese to help with a re-election campaign or by motivating voters to support the member," replied the professor. "If he doesn't get what he wants, he can direct cheese and voter support to the member's opponent in the next election. The more powerful the special interest rat, the harder he is to ignore. The result is that Council members are a lot less free to do what they think is right than any of us would like to believe. Ask any politician about all this catering to special interest rats, and he'll tell you that if he doesn't do it, some other rat will. It's the rare rat who will give up political power on principle."

"Amazing," said Conn.

"Amazingly unfortunate is maybe a better way of describing it," said Wonk. "Now, all this comes together at election time. Since most Council members will have done what the special interest rats wanted, they have plenty of campaign cheese at their disposal. They use this cheese to overwhelm opposing candidates with campaign ads and other publicity. It works so beautifully that almost no incumbent Council member loses a re-election effort."

Hedge and Conn sat in silence.

"You guys OK?" asked Wonk.

"Sorry, we're fine," stammered Hedge. "I'm beginning to see why Pol and Reform were so much different in office than what they promised during their initial campaigns."

"Well, get out your smelling salts," continued Wonk. "Rats have been quietly doing this kind of damage for a long time. The sheer volume of cheese that they've secured for themselves from the Council at the general public's expense boggles the mind. In my opinion, this is all part of a vast rat conspiracy that has infected Freedom Island. And I say this even though I'm a rat myself."

Wonk stopped pacing and paused briefly.

"What's important to see here is the vicious cycle that's been created. As special interest rats demand more from their Council members, these same Council members tax and spend more. As they tax and spend more, they become ever more attractive targets for special interest rats because they control so much cheese. Over time, these rats, and the population at large, look increasingly to the Council to provide some or all of the cheese they need."

"That last comment might be stretching things a bit, professor," said Conn.

"Maybe," answered Wonk, "but I hope you're appreciating my general point, which is that the Council is all about responding to well-connected rats, who are often strong enough to make or break political careers. The Council is not about solving the problems of the average animal."

Wonk turned and looked directly at Hedge. "So, Hedge, when you say that the rats are in the cheese, you're exactly right. And our political system is in danger as a result."

"These are great perspectives," said Hedge. "But as you point out, the problems we're discussing are not new problems. What solutions have been tried? And why have they failed?"

"Terrific questions," replied Wonk. "Despite its many recent problems, the Council has long strived to promote integrity and efficiency in government. Let me see if I can describe what they've attempted. Conn, do you have a blank poster I can borrow? If I put what I'm about to write on the chalkboard, we might lose it later if it gets erased."

"Certainly," said Conn, who happened to have some extra posters.

"One of the earliest measures they adopted was limits on spending," said Wonk as he wrote out 'Spending Limits.' "The Council, to its credit, wanted to constrain the runaway cheese spending that resulted from all of the influence peddling. They decided to pass rules to limit spending and borrowing. This effort quickly failed, however, because the rules weren't strong enough to help the Council resist the political forces demanding cheese."

Wonk wrote out the next point, 'Influence Limits.'

"Another idea they tried was to limit the influence of animals seeking cheese from the Council," continued Wonk. "They set up special rules to regulate their activities and require disclosure. These rules remain in effect today, but they've not constrained influence peddling in any meaningful way. I believe this is because there's so much cheese involved in politics. It would be like trying to stop a river. You can't, there's too much water."

Wonk wrote out yet another point, 'Campaign Limits.'

"The Council also tried to pass rules that limit spending in campaigns," continued Wonk, "with the idea being that you could reduce the impact of special interests by simply reducing the amount of cheese that could be spent on campaigns. Again, this didn't work because there's so much cheese in politics, but also because there's a belief that such limits restrict an animal's right to free speech, one of the most important Freedom Rules."

Wonk wrote out the next point, 'Tenure Limits.'

"The Council also tried limiting the amount of time rats can spend in office, believing that they would be less susceptible to outside influences if they could only run for reelection a few times. This hasn't worked either because, again, there's too much cheese in politics. Rats who want to get into the cheese always seem to find a way around any new limitation. They call it enlightened self-interest. I call it ratty behavior."

"Let me see if I can summarize where we are in this discussion," said Hedge. "First, there is an enormous amount of cheese in politics, and this cheese drives the behavior of rat politicians as well as outside rats trying to influence these politicians. Second, the Council, recognizing at least somewhat that there is value in government integrity and efficiency, has tried to pass laws that prevent rats from getting into the cheese. None of these measures has been effective. Third, there are a variety of reasons why these measures have failed, but one reason they have in common is that getting into the cheese is in the nature of every rat and is exceedingly difficult if not impossible to stop."

"I think that about sums it up," sighed the professor. "I've studied these problems for years, and sadly my conclusion is that there is very little that can be done to keep the rats out of the cheese. Eventually, it will be our undoing. Slowly, but surely, more and more cheese will accrue to the politicians and the well-connected. The rest of us will be stuck with high taxes, less freedom, and crushing debt. Eventually, we'll suffer the same fate as Animal Farm. Tyranny, albeit in a different form, will ultimately overwhelm us. I don't think it can be stopped."

"Maybe it can't," said Hedge, "but there's something I don't understand. It's true that the rats are in the cheese, but someone has to produce the cheese for these rats to get into, and it's the voters. Why aren't they doing something to stop all of this? Don't they have the power to do so?"

"Sure they do," replied the professor, "but they don't use it. And I think there are several reasons why. First, there's a sense of powerlessness. Many animals feel that their votes don't count. The rats have organized the spending and taxation so that there's never a clear up or down vote on anything that matters. As a result, average animals are gradually losing interest in elections. Nowadays, barely a majority of animals bother to vote. Even when they do get involved in Council elections and campaign hard for their candidates, nothing really changes, no matter who gets elected. The rats still end up in the cheese."

"We certainly felt powerless after we worked to elect a Limited Party majority," said Conn.

"The second reason," continued Wonk, "is that many ordinary animals are themselves compromised by all this cheese. The Council has been adept at making sure everyone perceives benefits from its actions to some degree. As a result, many animals end up supporting candidates or platforms that they largely don't like simply because of a few campaign promises to protect or expand particular benefits of interest to them. For example, Biz Rat will be inclined to support the candidate who promises the most cheese subsidies for his meadow projects, regardless of what other policies that candidate might endorse.

"A third reason," Wonk continued, "and this is very important, is that many animals who benefit from Council actions feel they are getting something for nothing."

"What do you mean by that?" inquired Hedge.

"Well," responded the professor, "it's hard to explain. I think, though, that it boils down to misaligned perceptions. Animals clearly perceive the benefits of cheese spending, but they don't perceive the cost. Sure, taxes are high, but the Council has set them up so that it's hard for individual taxpayers to feel the direct impact of additional spending. Some animals even see paying taxes as a benefit, since many overpay their taxes during the year and get a welcome cheese refund at year-end. In addition, the Council borrows vast amounts of cheese to make up tax shortfalls, which further obscures the costs of cheese spending. It's a terrible combination. Animals want the benefits the Council provides but don't feel the costs sufficiently, so they demand more and more. As I said, I think this will be our undoing."

There was a long silence as Hedge and Conn contemplated what the professor had said.

"You know," said Hedge, "I still think this problem can be solved."

"What do you mean, Hedge?" said Wonk.

"All of the solutions you described earlier failed because they were developed based on faulty thinking," replied Hedge. "There is another way."

VIII

Another way? I'm not sure I follow you," said the professor.
"The nature of the problem we face requires different thinking," replied Hedge.

"You've lost me, too, Hedge," said Conn.

"Let me see if I can explain with an example," said Hedge. "Many years ago, before the founding of Freedom Island, hedgehogs in the wild faced a variety of predators. None of these predators was more dangerous than the fox. Anytime my ancestors ventured away from home, they faced the near-certain prospect that a fox would try to have them for lunch. It was awful." Hedge shook his head sadly.

"Fortunately," he continued, his eyes brightening up, "nature provided us with an effective way to combat the fox, a defensive mechanism we hedgehogs call a hedgie."

"A hedgie?" said Wonk. "What's that?"

"I suppose I could describe it, but it's probably better just to show you," replied Hedge. "Watch this."

Time had not been particularly kind to Hedge. Though still a handsome hedgehog, he had put on some extra weight, and he lacked the vitality of his youth, which is why what happened next seemed all the more startling.

"Shoop!"

In the blink of an eye, the middle-aged, pleasantly plump Hedge snapped into the shape of a ball, his sharp spines protruding out in every direction. Wonk and Conn gasped at the sight of Hedge's sudden transformation, as neither realized that hedgehogs had this ability.

"Now," said Hedge, his muffled voice coming from somewhere among all those spines, "if either of you were a fox, do you think you'd be able to have me for lunch?"

Wonk and Conn didn't respond, still stunned by what they had seen. Slowly, Hedge unrolled from his spiny ball.

"I think we can keep the rats out of the cheese," continued Hedge as he straightened up fully, "but to do it, we need to develop a hedgie."

Wonk began to catch on to what Hedge was saying, and he smiled as he did. "I think I know where you're going with this," he said. "Previous solutions focused on specific actions and behaviors associated with rats getting into the cheese. These solutions failed because the always-clever rats would simply find ways around them."

"Exactly," said Hedge. "Hedgehogs have always known about this phenomenon. We discovered long ago that there's no rule you can impose on a fox that will prevent him from trying to have a tasty hedgehog for lunch. Trying to impose rules on rats to keep them out of the cheese is no different. It won't work. It can't work. We shouldn't even try."

"You're right, Hedge," said the professor. "Instead of complicated, piecemeal rules that are easy to circumvent, we need a simple defensive mechanism that is triggered automatically anytime the rats attempt to get into the cheese. Once we have it in place, we'll have a lot less to worry about."

"I love this idea," interjected Conn. "But I'm having trouble imagining what an effective hedgie will look like. If we're going to develop one, where do we start?"

"I think we start with the voters," replied Wonk. "After all, the rats are in the cheese because the voters allow it. And the reason they allow it is because they can't really see or feel what's happening. We need a hedgie that immediately affects large numbers of voters anytime too many rats get into too much cheese."

"I don't understand," said Conn. "The public knows that the rats are in the cheese. I'm sure I've read a dozen stories about outrageous waste, fraud, and abuse just in the last week. How can you claim that the voters can't really see or feel what's happening?"

"Good point, Conn," said Hedge. "But have you ever noticed how uninterested the public seems in all these stories?"

"I assumed that given the sheer volume, the public had simply become desensitized," said Conn.

"No," replied Hedge. "The real reason is because no one truly feels the impact of all this bad behavior at a personal level. Sure, there's transparency in the sense that everyone knows that the Council is up to no good, but the costs of what the Council is doing are not at all transparent. Wonk is right; we need a hedgie that generates voter awareness. To be more specific, we need a hedgie that makes the costs of rats getting in the cheese both obvious and painful to all. With this hedgie in place, whenever the Council gets out of hand and too many rats are in the cheese, animals will come together in sufficient numbers to demand that it stop. The question is, how do we design this hedgie?"

"Why don't we just develop a hedgie that restricts spending?" asked Conn.

"I don't think that will work," replied Wonk. "Spending involves so many priorities at so many different levels that it will be nearly impossible to formulate a simple spending-based hedgie that can stand the test of time. Instead, I think we need to create a hedgie that works through the tax system."

"That sounds right," said Hedge. "After all, if we want to ensure that voters feel the effects of more spending, then we literally have to make them pay every time spending increases. What better way to do this than through taxes?"

"Absolutely," said Wonk. "And you make an important point. A critical design feature will be a clear linkage between spending and taxation. In other words, any change in spending should trigger an immediate change in taxation."

"Of course, the average animal is already paying taxes," added Hedge, "so we're going to need a clever plan that focuses their attention when spending gets excessive. We also need to be sure that once animals are focused, they can take effective action at the polls."

"I agree," said Wonk. "The way to do this will be to require the Council to balance spending and taxing, which will ensure that any time cheese spending exceeds cheese tax revenue, a tax increase kicks in."

"Didn't the Council try to do something like this once before?" asked Conn. "I remember them passing a balanced budget rule. I don't believe they've balanced the budget since."

"I think we're talking about something with more teeth," said Wonk. "What we need is a new Freedom Rule that says spending must be balanced with taxes. We wouldn't be stipulating how much the Council could spend; frankly, they could spend as much as they wanted. We'd just require that when they did increase spending, voters would automatically pay higher taxes. This way, a voter could go to the polls with something meaningful to decide. If he accepts the higher taxes, he can continue supporting candidates who want to spend more. If he thinks taxes are too high, he can support a candidate who favors less spending. It's that simple."

"With a system like this in place, rats won't be able to hide the fact that they're getting into more cheese," said Conn. "Voters will know this is going on because they will feel the pain of higher taxes."

"Precisely," said Wonk.

"Here's a harder question," said Hedge. "How do we ensure that enough animals feel these costs through higher taxes? It's important that everyone is affected. Otherwise, there won't be enough motivated voters to keep the spending in check."

"The more animals who end up paying higher taxes as a result of more spending, the better," replied the professor.

"I agree," said Conn. "But we should exempt the lowest 15% of all cheese earners from any taxation whatsoever. Poor Church Mice who currently pay pension and medical taxes shouldn't be paying any taxes at all. By exempting them from taxation entirely, we'll be helping them economically, and they'll in turn feel like they're being treated fairly."

"Definitely," said Hedge. "Focusing taxes only on the top 85% seems fair and reasonable. But I worry that it's going to be really hard for this group to feel a spending-driven tax increase under our current system. There are simply too many different taxes. Which ones will go up when an increase is required? Some of them? All of them?"

"I think we're going to have to consolidate all of these different taxes," speculated Wonk. "We'll need to eliminate all current forms of taxation except cheese income taxes. And for this one remaining tax, there should be ideally just a single rate that applies equally to the top 85% of cheese earners. My guess is that a rate of about 22% will be enough to cover current spending levels."

"What's the advantage of a single rate tax?" asked Conn.

"A single rate will be highly visible," replied Wonk. "Everyone will know the rate, and everyone will know when the Council changes the rate to pay for extra spending. Applying the same rate equally means that fully 85% of the income-earning population will be affected anytime the Council has to increase taxes to pay for the rats being in the cheese. No preferences, manipulations, or deductions will be available to avoid the tax, and no one will be able to manipulate the system for unfair advantage like they do today. It won't take but a few tax increases before animals start voting for spending reform."

"That's great," said Conn. "Imagine this pre-election headline: 'Council raises the tax rate from 22% to 25% to cover large spending increases.' With such a headline impacting 85% of the income-earning voters, you can bet that the Council elections will be affected."

"I see another, more subtle benefit," said Wonk. "Over time, it will bring about a mindset change in the general public. Today, when it comes to new spending, too many animals ask 'what's in it for me?' Under our plan, animals will instead be asking 'how much are my taxes going to go up?' Sure, it's not a perfect plan, and it won't eliminate all instances of outrageous spending or corruption, but it should help a lot. It's important that we not allow the perfect to be the enemy of the good."

"I have a question, professor," asked Hedge. "Would our single rate tax apply to entities other than individual animals? For example, Biz Rat has a company that specializes in big projects. Spotless Rat runs the Clean Island foundation. Rich Rat provides cheese to several major charities. Preacher Rat has a big church. How will our plan affect these organizations?"

"I think the idea should be to treat every animal and every organization exactly the same," replied Wonk. "There's no doubt that it will be very hard for some animals to accept the idea that charities and churches should be taxed just like individuals. In fact, a final form of our plan might well include some compromises that exclude certain types of organizations from the single rate tax. But, in my opinion, we should start with a pure system that treats everyone the same. And the reason for this is compelling. The more individuals and entities that are treated the same, the more effective our tax hedgie will be at keeping the rats out of the cheese, and the harder it will be for anyone to manipulate the taxes they pay. To be successful, our proposal must make the tax system as simple as possible, but not simpler."

"Here's another question," said Hedge. "You mentioned consolidating all existing taxes. That's a pretty big leap. Is such a thing possible?"

"Nothing is ever easy," replied Wonk. "And you're right, it is a big leap. Our proposal would replace nearly every existing tax with a single rate tax. Since taxes are such a significant part of everyone's financial planning and thinking, a major change like this will have to be considered carefully and probably phased in over time. But I think once animals understand the goal of our plan, the pain of implementing it will be easier to endure."

"I like all this so far," said Conn, "but I'm still worried about fairness. It's good that we've exempted the bottom 15% of taxpayers, but what about the wealthy? A 22% rate seems awfully low for them. Shouldn't they pay more?"

"The current top tax rates are already much higher than 22%," responded Hedge. "Many of the new and up-and-coming rich pay these current high rates, but the really rich don't because of all the deductions, exemptions and special treatments available to them. Animals like Rich Rat can manipulate their affairs to avoid paying any taxes at all. The important point is that truly wealthy animals can control their taxable income, whereas average and up-and-coming animals can't."

"Great point," replied Conn. "I can see how a single rate tax with no exemptions, applied equally to all entities and individuals as well as all types of income, will force every animal above a certain cheese income level to pay tax. This will ensure that animals with a lot of cheese income can't escape paying tax as some of them do now. But what about animals who have a lot of cheese already? Under your proposal, Rich Rat won't have to pay tax on the massive amount of cheese he already has. It seems to me that we should create some provision to tax animals who currently have large amounts of cheese but show very little income. If we don't, Fairness Rat and others like her will oppose our overall idea. I think we must re-introduce some of the tax progressivity that we lost by moving toward a single rate tax."

"You raise a very reasonable point," said Wonk. "I think we can address this by adopting an asset tax, which is something I've thought about for a long time."

"How would an asset tax work, professor?" asked Hedge.

"Income taxes tax cheese as you earn it," replied Wonk. "Asset taxes tax cheese you already have. We don't have a real asset tax currently, but a close relative to it is the estate tax."

"You mean the taxes that are paid when you die?" asked Conn.

"That's right," replied Wonk. "A true asset tax would work the same way, except that it would be collected every year, and at a much lower rate."

"Wouldn't such a tax be complicated to administer?" asked Hedge.

"Yes," replied Wonk. "But because most cheese on Freedom Island is controlled by relatively few animals, like Rich Rat, the tax can be structured so that only the top 10% of the asset holders pay the tax. This will minimize the cost of administration and focus collection efforts on animals and entities that have a lot of assets. One thing to point out, however, is that such a tax can be dangerous. Since it will apply to so few animals, it will be easy to get a majority vote to raise it. So, it should have a very low rate, probably 1% or less, and the maximum rate as well as the percentage of taxpayers who pay the tax should be specifically limited in a new Freedom Rule."

"Wouldn't an asset tax be criticized as just a 'soak the rich' scheme?" asked Hedge.

"There is no question that the impact of this tax must be analyzed carefully," replied Wonk. "But it isn't a soak the rich scheme. Some well-to-do animals who will pay the new asset tax may in fact end up paying lower overall taxes than they do currently. Instead, I would characterize the asset tax as a 'soak large concentrations of cheese sitting around' scheme. Individual animals, big trusts, major foundations, or any other entity with large accumulations of cheese will be brought into the tax system. The result will be a lower overall tax rate, which will help animals who are working hard and trying to earn a living."

"I like this," said Conn. "It will help overcome one of the biggest problems with our current system, which is that it allows animals like Rich Rat to manipulate their affairs to avoid paying their fair share of the tax burden."

"There's another important benefit," said Wonk. "Even a small asset tax should raise a considerable amount of revenue. This new revenue can be used to keep the single income tax rate low. If it works out like I think it will, the rate will be low enough to ensure that a clear majority of taxpayers end up paying less taxes under our plan than they do currently. This will help generate the political support we need to get our plan to become law."

"Maybe we should try to summarize our discussion so far," suggested Hedge.

"Good idea," said Wonk. "At my age, I might forget some of this unless we write it down. Let me first see if I can compose a clear statement of the problem we're trying to solve."

Wonk sat down at his big table and began to write on another one of Conn's blank posters. Conn seemed to have an endless supply.

The rats have been in the cheese for a long time, but the problem has grown more serious and threatens the stability and financial integrity of our government.

- **Cheese spending that benefits special interest rats but that would never command a majority vote of all animals is rapidly growing.**
- **The complex tax system in place to cover this spending is increasingly inadequate and distributes the tax burden unfairly, enabling many animals to escape paying their fair share.**

Everyone knows the rats are in the cheese. For several reasons, however, this problem is particularly resistant to solutions.

- First, the rats have conspired to make sure that the cost of excessive cheese spending does not affect individual animals directly. The result is that animals don't feel a need to take real action.
- Second, many animals feel powerless to take action anyway. Even when they do elect politicians who promise change, these politicians inevitably fail to deliver. As a result, many animals are convinced that their votes no longer matter.
- Lastly, and most seriously, many animals are in the cheese themselves to some degree. They fear any proposal that might affect whatever cheese benefit they receive, however small, and they complain loudly at the prospect of even the mildest change. After all, there's a little rat in every animal.

To get the rats out of the cheese, we require some new thinking. What we need is a hedgie, a fool-proof mechanism that reacts automatically when too many rats get into too much cheese.

"This is great, professor," said Conn. "Let me see if I can follow your problem statement with a description of our hedgie as it stands now." He took the pencil from Wonk and started writing on another poster.

We believe that an effective hedgie should have the following three attributes:

1) A Freedom Rule that requires cheese spending to be matched by cheese taxes

2) A single rate cheese income tax that replaces all existing taxes and is applied equally to the top 85% of all individuals and organizations above a certain income level

3) An asset tax applied to the top 10% of asset concentrations with a rate capped in a special Freedom Rule

"What do you think?" asked Conn.

"I think you've captured our proposed hedgie pretty well," said Hedge.

"The more I think about it, the more I'm convinced this plan can work," said Wonk. "Our proposal will restore transparency in the tax system, and voters will once again be confident that everyone is being treated equally, one of the first things the founders wrote into our Freedom Rules."

"I'm excited, too" said Hedge, "but do our proposals have any chance of enactment?"

"Even though it's likely that a majority of voters will be better off under our plan, we must not underestimate the strength or the resourcefulness of the rats who will oppose what we're advocating," replied the professor. "The rich and other well-connected rats will hate our plan with a passion since it will greatly restrict their ability to game the system for their own benefit."

"You're right about the likely opposition, professor," said Hedge. "So before we go any further, we need to pressure test these ideas. We need to subject them to some pretty tough skepticism. We need to make sure that we can answer even the harshest criticism."

"Well," said Conn, "I can't think of a better way to do this than with our policy group back home. If our ideas can survive a session with Animals for Honest Government, we'll be ready to face anyone on Freedom Island."

"Professor," said Hedge, "do you have some time to help us out? Between the three of us, I'll bet we can clearly explain and defend what we're proposing."

"Time?" exclaimed Wonk. "I'm retired! I have all the time in the world! Besides, I wouldn't miss this for anything."

"Great," said Hedge. "We'll head back home first thing in the morning."

IX

Hedge didn't sleep much that night. Though excited about the ideas that he, Conn, and Wonk had developed, he worried about the tough questions they were likely to get from the policy group. Would their hedgie stand up to harsh scrutiny?

Daybreak finally came, and Hedge was the first to venture outside. Gentle sunshine bathed the riverbank, illuminating just a hint of morning fog over the calm waters. Perhaps the serenity of the moment was a sign that the coming debates would be easy. Perhaps not.

"Good morning," said Wonk, startling Hedge a bit with his greeting.

"Hello, professor," replied Hedge. "Is Conn ready to go?"

"Sound asleep," said Wonk.

"Since he's not awake yet, let's talk for a few minutes," said Hedge.

"What's on your mind, Hedge?" said Wonk.

"I have a question about a point you made earlier," said Hedge. "You said that rats in the cheese might lead one day to a return of the tyranny that plagued Animal Farm. I agree with you, but as I think about it, I just can't see our society succumbing to a dictatorship. It just doesn't seem possible."

"The most important thing to understand about tyranny," replied Wonk, "is that it comes in many forms. Sometimes it's obvious, sometimes it's not so obvious. Sometimes it's easy to identify and correct, sometimes not."

Hedge's spines bristled a bit as he heard Wonk's words, remembering that Preacher Rat had said exactly the same thing earlier.

"In the early history of Animal Farm," continued the professor, "animals suffered greatly under Farmer Jones, who mistreated them and denied them even the most basic freedoms. In my view, it was a Tyranny of Slavery. As we know, the animals overthrew Farmer Jones and created their own society, in which all animals were equal. Unfortunately, they didn't design a system that prevented the accumulation of too much power among just a few animals. In time, Napoleon and the other pigs amassed so much power that they were able to rule over the other animals, rendering their votes and their voices impotent. Animal Farm became a Tyranny of Dictatorship."

"Makes sense to me," said Hedge. "I've thought along these lines for some time."

"On Freedom Island," continued Wonk, "we formed a free society. We carefully enshrined our Freedom Rules and made them hard to change, thus ensuring that we would always have the basic freedoms and protections so grossly violated on Animal Farm by Napoleon and the other pigs. Over time, our system has worked well, and our society has prospered."

"But now," said Hedge picking up the train of thought, "oppression seems to be returning. Ever so slowly, the basic freedoms enshrined in our Freedom Rules, which the founders designed to avoid the mistakes made on Animal Farm, are becoming less secure. And the reason is because the rats are in the cheese. As a result, we have tyranny emerging in a new form—a Tyranny of Well-Connected Rats."

"I think you're correct," said Wonk.

"I just hope that our hedgie is the right antidote for this new kind of tyranny," said Hedge. "It should work. It's a direct shot at the strength of the rats—their cheese connection."

"Hedge, if you can get that point across," said Wonk, "I think the voters will support your plan."

"I hope so," replied Hedge. "But if we don't get going, we'll never get the chance to find out."

"Time to wake up Conn from his beauty sleep," said the professor.

"I'll take care of that!" said Hedge energetically. He walked over to the window of the room where Conn was snoring away.

"C'mon, Conn, get with the program," shouted Hedge. "We've got a long journey ahead of us!"

"All right, I'm coming," mumbled Conn. After a bit of rustling, Conn emerged, still not quite awake. "You guys kept me up past my bedtime," he moaned

"How could you sleep anyway?" said Hedge. "With all of our new ideas, I could hardly sleep myself!"

"Maybe you can stay awake all night," replied Conn, "but mice need their sleep."

"Sleep is for the weak," said Hedge. "Let's go!"

The trio began their journey, with the conversation turning quickly to the coming debate.

"What sort of questions do you think the group will pose?" asked Conn as they hiked across a meadow.

"I think we can expect all sorts of questions, and frankly criticisms," replied Hedge.

"I agree," added Wonk. "As I mentioned before, there are a lot of animals who are tied to the status quo. Convincing them of the need for change will be difficult."

"Here's something I bet they'll ask," said Conn. Hedge and Wonk listened as Conn outlined his question.

"Well," replied Wonk, "I'd answer your question this way...."

For the next several days, the three companions worked through the questions they thought they might hear from the policy group. As they made their way across the island, Hedge grew more confident that things would go well and that they would be able to answer any concerns the policy group might have.

After three quick days, they arrived back at Hedge's place.

"That trip seemed to go by pretty fast," remarked Wonk.

"It did, but we don't have much daylight left today," replied Hedge. "We need to get the word out quickly about a meeting of Animals for Honest Government tonight. Conn, will you work your magic?"

"Can do," said Conn. "I'll get started now and meet you back at the lodge hall at sundown."

***

A substantial crowd showed up that night, packing the hall beyond its limits.

"Incredible," remarked Wonk.

"What do you mean?" inquired Hedge.

"How was Conn able to pull together such a large group so quickly?" said Wonk. "There must be a hundred animals here."

"Conn's networks know no bounds!" said Hedge, laughing. "No one can spread the word like he can."

Just then, Conn walked up. "Hedge, I think we're ready. Care to get things started?"

"You bet," said Hedge. He turned and stepped up onto a platform in the middle of the hall.

"My friends," boomed Hedge in his crowd-stopping voice. A few seconds later, the hall was quiet enough for Hedge to resume. "Thanks for coming on such short notice," he continued. "As we told you we would at our last meeting, Conn and I left town to pay a visit to Professor Wonk."

As Hedge spoke, Conn took out the poster with the problem summary that the group had developed at the last meeting. He put it on a wooden stand so that everyone could see it.

The Rats are in the Cheese
1. Council actions promote inequality before the law
2. Our complex taxes cheat average animals
3. We do vote for the Council, but the Council takes many actions that a majority of us would never support

"After some lengthy debates," Hedge continued, "we came up with some additional thinking and new ideas, which we'd like to share with you tonight. Importantly, we'll want to hear your reactions and questions."

"Don't worry, Hedge!" shouted someone. "Have you ever known us to hold back?"

"Now that you mention it, no!" said Hedge, chuckling. "All right, to help get things going, I'd like to introduce Professor Wonk, who came back with us to help with our presentation tonight. Professor?"

A quick round of applause and a few cheers ensued as the professor stepped up to the platform.

"Thanks, Hedge," said the professor. During their trip, Hedge, Conn, and Wonk had developed a plan to present their ideas. They agreed that Wonk would speak first, followed by Hedge.

"Before we take your questions, I'd like to do two things," continued Wonk. "First, I'm going to offer some additional thinking on the original problem summary that Conn just put up here. Next, Hedge is going to outline our proposed solution. Sound all right to you?"

Murmurs resonated through the hall, with the words "yes" and "go for it" clearly understandable.

"Terrific," he continued. Wonk began to recap the overall challenge, repeating many of the same points he had made before with Hedge and Conn. "So when Hedge says that the rats are in the cheese," he summarized at one point, "he's exactly right. And our prosperity and freedom are in danger as a result."

Again, murmurs resonated through the hall, with everyone seemingly in agreement with the professor's assessment.

"I've tried to summarize the problem in writing," continued the professor. "Conn, could you put up the poster I wrote out the other day?"

Wonk stepped to the side as Conn pulled out Wonk's poster and displayed it on the same wooden stand, replacing the poster he had put there earlier. Wonk then read through each point. He emphasized his belief that out-of-control spending did not command majority support and that the tax system to support such spending was unfair. He also highlighted why this problem seemed so hard to resolve, pointing out that animals don't sense the danger, don't feel they can take effective action in any case, and are themselves compromised in some way by Council cheese.

"As my summary states," he concluded, "we need to try new thinking. We need a fool-proof mechanism that reacts automatically to protect us when too many rats get into too much cheese. What we need is a hedgie, which Hedge is going to describe."

"Professor," said a chipmunk on one side of the room, "this seems a little complicated. Can you boil it all down a bit?"

Wonk paused for a few seconds.

"Basically," he said gesturing to the chipmunk, "the voters have grown too weak. Let me see if I can show you what I mean."

Conn brought up another poster for Wonk to write on.

"Try this on for size," said Wonk as he began to draw.

"What I'm attempting to draw here is a three-legged stool. One leg represents spending, one leg represents taxation and the third leg represents the voters. The rats sitting on the stool are eating the cheese that they have managed to acquire from the rest of us. When the system is operating well, the voters control and restrain rat behavior and the amount of cheese they get into through taxing and spending."

Wonk asked Conn to put up a blank poster. Wonk drew the same picture again, but with some important modifications.

"Over time, as Freedom Island has gotten richer, things have changed. Now the stool looks like this." Wonk's new sketch showed the same stool, but with a shriveled voter leg and fat spending and taxation legs. The top of the stool was much bigger and covered with rats dancing around a much larger amount of cheese.

"We think the rats have weakened the voter leg to the point that voters can no longer effectively restrain the rats," said Wonk. "They still let us go to the polls, but we no longer have up-or-down votes that mean anything, with the result that spending and taxation are increasingly out of control. The risk we face is that the weight of the rats and the cheese they get into will crush the voter leg, and our whole system of government will topple."

"Those dirty rats!" yelled one animal. But he was a rat himself, so he self-consciously sat back down.

"When you look at this second sketch," continued the professor, "it's easy to see why nothing we've tried that might restrain the rats has worked. Without a strong voter leg, the rats promptly find a way around these measures."

The hall was quiet for several moments. Wonk turned to Hedge.

"Hedge," he said, "I think we've got them where we want them. Why don't you describe how we propose to solve this problem?"

"Thank you, professor," said Hedge as he stepped forward. Hedge then launched into a description of a hedgie. Like he did with Conn and Wonk, he startled everyone by snapping into a spiny ball to demonstrate the concept. He then outlined the key elements of the hedgie they had developed, explaining how each one would work.

"In summary," he concluded, "our hedgie contains the following three elements. First, rats shouldn't be able to hide the fact that they're in the cheese, so we need a Freedom Rule that requires cheese spending to be matched by cheese taxes. Second, so that a broad constituency can form to get the rats out of the cheese, we need a single rate cheese income tax that replaces all existing taxes and is applied equally to the top 85% of all individuals and organizations that earn income. And third, to promote fairness and ensure that the asset rich, not just the income rich, bear a fair and reasonable share of the tax burden, we need an asset tax with a capped rate that is applied to all asset concentrations above a certain level. We think that a hedgie with these three features will help get the rats out of the cheese and go a long way toward restoring integrity and efficiency in our government."

As Hedge spoke, Conn displayed the three hedgie elements, which Hedge had written out earlier during the meeting with Wonk.

We believe that an effective hedgie should have the following three attributes:

1) A Freedom Rule that requires cheese spending to be matched by cheese taxes

2) A single rate cheese income tax that replaces all existing taxes and is applied equally to the top 85% of all individuals and organizations above a certain income level

3) An asset tax applied to the top 10% of asset concentrations with a rate capped in a special Freedom Rule

Wonk slowly stepped back up onto the platform as Hedge finished his remarks, followed by Conn.

"That's our proposal," said Conn enthusiastically. "What do you think? What questions do you have?"

It wasn't long before paws started to go up.

"Let's start with the idea of forcing a balanced budget," asked a goat in front. "I understand that requiring spending to be balanced by taxation shines a bright light on rats in the cheese. But why do we need a Freedom Rule to accomplish this? If we enshrine fiscal balance in a Freedom Rule, won't that unduly restrict the Council's spending authority in an emergency?"

"The reason we need a constitutional amendment is to eliminate what I would call wiggle room," replied Wonk. "Remember that one way rats keep other animals from really feeling that the rats are in the cheese is by borrowing instead of taxing. We need to take away their ability to do this. You do raise a good point about emergencies, though. As I think about it, I don't see why we can't include a provision that allows temporary deficit cheese spending if, say, four-fifths of Council members certify that an emergency exists, or something like that."

"I'm not sure I like the idea of a single rate tax," interjected Nutsy Squirrel. As the resident group skeptic, he always asked the toughest questions. Hedge shifted uncomfortably as Nutsy spoke.

"Why do we need a single rate?" he continued. "Our current, multi-rate tax system is progressive, meaning that the income rich, who have more disposable income, take on a higher burden relative to the less rich. Isn't that fair?"

"The current system has so many exceptions and exclusions that the really rich aren't paying the top rates anyway," replied Hedge. "When you take into account the pension taxes, many animals of modest means are paying higher rates than animals who earn more. But as to your question, the main reasons for a single rate tax that applies to 85% of taxpayers are threefold. First, when the Council spends more, fully 85% of the income-earning population will feel the effect though an adjustment to the single rate. We're convinced that this will unify animals and create a powerful constituency for keeping spending under control. Second, a single rate with no exclusions ensures that no one escapes paying their fair share, not even the rich. Animals will no longer be able to get tax relief by influencing the Council to give them special breaks. The only way they'll be able to get their taxes lowered is if the Council reduces spending. Lastly, we do preserve progressivity by establishing an asset tax for wealthy individuals and entities. We also do it by excluding the bottom 15% of income earners from any tax. That's much better than what we have today, in which even the poorest church mouse pays a pension tax on the first ounce of cheese she earns. What's fair about that?"

"All right," Nutsy continued. "But here's another concern. I worry about your idea that all entities should be taxed the same. Do you really mean to say that charities, nonprofits, and even churches should pay taxes?"

"I realize that shifting to a single rate tax that applies equally to every individual and entity will create some pain," replied Hedge. "Many animals and organizations will resist giving up the special exceptions and exclusions they have. But keep in mind what we'll get as a society in return. We'll have a system that can't be tinkered with. The rich won't be able to organize their affairs to avoid taxes. The middle class will stop spending so much time thinking about deductions. Since tax avoidance and outright evasion will be greatly reduced, animals will once again feel that that we have a fair system in which everyone is paying their fair share. This should go a long way toward restoring integrity in our government."

"Won't charities and nonprofits get hit twice with your proposal?" asked Nutsy, continuing his cross examination. "Not only will they have to pay taxes, but the contributions they receive won't be tax deductible for the donors. Won't these organizations fail as result?"

"No doubt some will in the short run," replied Hedge. "But our sense is that in the long run, charities will remain important to many animals. The entire welfare system was supported by charitable contributions before we had income taxes. Besides, the notion of public charity is deeply embedded in the fabric of our collective conscience."

Hedge looked out over the crowd.

"To prove my point, let's take a quick poll," he continued. "Anyone who thinks animals will turn their backs on the needy or the worthy just because they don't get a tax deduction for charitable contributions, please raise a paw."

No one did.

"I thought as much," said Hedge. "But you're right, Nutsy, that some charities will take a hit, so we need to phase this in slowly. Again, keep in mind what we get in return: a tax system that can't be tinkered with and a restored sense among the public that the tax system is fair and equitable."

"Did you consider a consumption tax or a broad-based sales tax?" continued Nutsy.

"I've done considerable research on consumption-based tax systems," replied Wonk. "There are several problems with these systems. First, it's almost impossible to ensure that all sales are included in the tax. The pressure to exclude items like food and medicine is strong and constant. Each exclusion drives the overall rate up, and above a certain level, cheating becomes overwhelming. Second, the tax is regressive. In these systems, the poor end up paying a higher fraction of their income than the rich. Some proponents have attempted to correct this problem but at the expense of tremendous additional complexity. Third, we don't really have the tax collection infrastructure for a consumption tax like we do for an income tax. We'd have to invest a lot of cheese to create such infrastructure. Lastly, any time other societies have introduced consumption taxes, they've ended up being in addition to rather than in place of income taxes. The result has always been higher overall taxes, and a diminished linkage between taxation and spending."

"Here's another question," said Nutsy. "If your single rate tax is implemented, who will end up paying more taxes? Who will pay less?"

"My guess is that anyone who has structured his or her affairs to avoid taxes significantly is going to pay a lot more," replied the professor. "This probably includes the really rich as well as maybe some who are less well off. These animals won't like our proposal one bit. But why shouldn't they pay taxes like everyone else? After all, fair is fair. The good news is that bringing these animals into the tax system will result in a lower overall rate for everyone else."

"One last question about your single rate tax," said Nutsy. "It's true that our current tax system has a lot of subsidies, exemptions, and exclusions. But the Council adopted these by and large for legitimate reasons, like supporting an economically depressed area, or providing relief to storm victims, or encouraging critical investments. Won't your single rate eliminate tax system support for important things like this?"

"Absolutely," replied Hedge. Nutsy frowned and raised his paw as if to protest.

"But hold on," interrupted Hedge. "We're not saying that we shouldn't support groups or activities that need support. We're just saying that we shouldn't do it through the tax code. Instead, we should do it through spending. The Council should feel free to support as many groups with as much spending as it wants. In the end, this additional spending will translate through the balanced budget requirement into an increase in the single rate tax that the top 85% of income earners pay. The taxpayers will decide whether this is acceptable and vote accordingly. If the overall spending gets out of hand, animals will feel it, and they'll vote for Council members with different priorities. This is the key to our hedgie. It will empower voters to keep rats out of the cheese, and it will restore a collective feeling that votes really do count. What could be better for our democracy?"

Nutsy nodded his head in agreement.

"Keep in mind also that while a lot of the tax breaks you allude to seem legitimate, many are really just underhanded ways that the rats use to get into the cheese," said Wonk. "This needs to be stopped."

"I'm starting to like your proposals," admitted Nutsy.

"We think most animals will," replied Hedge. "In fact, let's try another quick poll. OK everyone, think for a minute about your own cheese income last year, and how much in total taxes you paid, including the pension tax. Now multiply your income before all the complicated deductions and exclusions by our estimated rate of 22%. Who pays less tax?"

After a few seconds of mental math, almost all the animals raised their paws.

"How is it possible that nearly everyone here will pay less taxes, but at the same time the Council will raise the same amount of revenue, as you suggest they will, with a single rate of 22%?" asked Nutsy.

"There are two answers," replied Hedge. "First, the asset tax will raise a lot of revenue from those who have successfully finessed the current system to avoid taxes. Second, there are no well-connected rats here tonight. I'm pretty sure none of them will pay lower taxes under our plan. It is for these two reasons that I think what we're proposing will resonate with a majority of voters."

"Speaking of the asset tax," said Conn, "does anyone have any questions about it?"

"I do," replied a gerbil way in the back. "Why do you have a limit on the asset tax for the super rich? The rate should be higher than 1% for them."

"It's easy for an asset tax to get out of hand, particularly since it would apply to so few animals or organizations," replied Wonk. "If we're not careful, this kind of tax could be very destructive. Remember, we're proposing it because it balances the single rate tax with more progressivity, which to Nutsy's earlier point is important. In addition, it ensures that large concentrations of assets will begin to bear some of the tax burden, something we also think is important. But animals shouldn't view the asset tax as a populist, soak-the-rich scheme. It isn't."

"What about the estate tax?" asked a portly hen near the exit. "Why shouldn't we keep this tax?"

"The estate tax is viewed by many as unfair, with some even referring to it as a death tax," replied the professor. "In addition, the estate tax rates are pretty high and often force families to break up businesses they've worked years to build. We think it's better and easier for these well-off animals to pay a very small asset tax each year rather than a huge, one-time, death-triggered estate tax. Besides, one thing I've noticed about the estate tax is that somehow the really big estates never seem to get broken up when the tax is triggered. The reason, of course, is that the really rich have the resources and connections to structure their estates to avoid the tax. We believe that a small asset tax collected each year will be less lucrative to avoid and, in time, much easier to collect."

Hedge broke in at this point, sensing that they had done an effective job at answering everyone's concerns.

"Let me ask a question," he interjected. "What does everyone think about our proposals overall? Are they starting to make sense? Do you support them?"

A lone animal started clapping. It was Nutsy Squirrel. After a second or two, others joined in. Soon, the entire group was cheering.

"You're really onto something here," said Nutsy as the applause died down. "What's the next step? Where do you go from here?"

"I think we need to keep testing our proposals," replied Hedge.

"Agreed," said Wonk. "We should spend time with some Council members to get their reaction."

"I have a better idea," suggested Conn. "Let's go see Fixer Rat. He's a political operator who holds several important Council staff jobs. He knows the political scene better than anyone I've met."

The meeting ended, and Hedge, Conn, and Wonk stepped down from the platform to mingle with the crowd. No one there could remember the last time they had all been so enthusiastic or excited. It was electrifying!

X

The next day, Hedge, Conn, and Wonk paid a visit to Council Headquarters. Conn had no trouble securing a quick meeting with Fixer Rat, who was glad to see a long-time friend.

Fixer was a small rat, with piercing eyes, slick hair, and a confident demeanor. He earned his name as a youngster by developing a reputation for being able to fix just about anything. Though his career as a handyman soon gave way to politics, he managed to preserve his reputation as a "fixer." These days, however, getting "fixed" by Fixer wasn't always a happy experience.

Over the years, Fixer had developed into one of the strongest Limited Party political operators on Freedom Island. As a Council staffer rather than a Council member, his work entailed campaign fund-raising from well-connected rats, manipulation of voting blocs and voter perceptions, and ensuring that his many political connections benefited from Council decision-making as much as possible. On several occasions, Conn had inadvertently introduced Fixer to some powerful animals, many of whom became big-time contributors to Fixer's various schemes.

"Conn!" exclaimed Fixer as Conn, Hedge, and Wonk stepped into his office. "It's great to see you. How do you like my new plaque?"

Fixer proudly picked up a large, framed sign that rested prominently on his desk. It read, 'Show me the Cheese.'

"It cuts out all the uncomfortable small talk and gets right to the point," continued Fixer. "I'm convinced that it has magical powers. In fact, that last big-wig you sent my way donated a mountain of cheese to one Councilmember's upcoming campaign, and I hardly had to say a word!"

Conn shook his head, realizing that he had contributed to creating a political monster.

"I can't wait to hear what you've brought me today," said Fixer loudly, slapping Conn on the back. "Who are your friends? Are they rich? Did they bring any cheese?"

"Hang on, Fixer," interjected Conn. "I'm afraid I'm not here to supply you with yet another wealthy connection. I am hoping, however, that you'll listen to some ideas we have. These are my good friends Hedge and Wonk, and they're here to help explain what we're thinking. We're hoping you can give us some insightful reactions."

"Any new idea that can help me move cheese to my side of the table has my full attention," said Fixer.

"You might be a little disappointed in what you're about to hear," said Conn. "Hedge, would you care to describe our proposals?"

Hedge mentioned the Animals for Honest Government policy group, briefly reviewed the problem of rats in the cheese and outlined the hedgie they had developed.

"We want to explore what it will take to get our proposal in front of the Council," he said in conclusion. "We'd like your advice on what to do next."

"My advice would be to toss all this nonsense in the trash and go home," said Fixer, clearly unimpressed and even a little testy. "You're wasting your time and mine."

"What?" exclaimed Hedge. "What do you mean?"

"Let's see," replied Fixer. "How about a quick vote count? Oops! Sorry, your proposals just got zero Council votes. Nada. Zip. Zilch."

"I don't understand!" said an outraged Hedge. "How can you say this?"

"Before you get upset, Hedgie-boy, let me explain life to you," replied Fixer sharply. "The Council is all about cheese. Council members, and all the animals who deal with the Council, focus exclusively on cheese and the power that such cheese generates. So, when it comes to legislation, the overriding question is, does such legislation generate power and cheese? Your proposal not only doesn't do this but will likely take a lot of power and cheese out of the system. No Council members will support such a proposal for the simple reason that they can't afford to. If they did, they'd immediately lose support from well-connected rats focused on getting cheese from the Council. They'd be out of office in a heartbeat. Conn, you know better than to bring me a goofy plan like this. Are you out of your mind?"

"We understand that our proposal will affect some pretty powerful interests," said Conn. "But we believe that many animals will support it."

"You're dreaming," said Fixer. "This proposal won't get off the ground without Council support. Conn, you know I love you, baby, but take this plan back to your policy pinheads and have a bonfire. In its place, why don't you guys think up something that will generate more Council cheese?"

Hedge could barely contain himself, but somehow he managed.

"I think we're done here," he said tersely.

Fixer couldn't resist one last slap.

"Remember, Hedgie-boy," said Fixer tauntingly, "it's all about the cheese! Cheese, cheese, cheese! Just say 'yes' to cheese, and you'll feel better!"

Hedge jumped up from his chair and stormed out of Fixer's office. Wonk and Conn quickly followed, catching up with him at the end of the hall where all of the Council member offices were located. Hedge was furious.

"Fixer is nothing but a political hack!" he exclaimed.

"No kidding," said Conn.

Just then, the door to one of the Council member offices swung open, and out walked a very cheerful Phat Mouse and several of his suspicious companions.

"Phat?" said Conn, surprised. "What are you doing here?"

"I've just met with one of my new best friends," replied Phat, happily. "I got a call from Fixer right after I met with you guys. He agreed to introduce me to a pliable Council member who could get me the help I need for my latest cheese scheme!"

"This day is getting worse by the minute," said Hedge.

"You should have taken me up on my offer, Conn," continued Phat. "I could have made you rich!"

"What you're doing is wrong, Phat," replied Conn.

"Whatever," said Phat dismissively to Conn as he walked back toward Fixer's office. "Besides, Fixer has all the contacts I need. You won't have to worry anymore about tarnishing your precious reputation by introducing your friends to the likes of me, Mr. Straight-Laced. Have a nice day."

***

Hedge, Conn, and Wonk walked slowly out of the Council headquarters. After a short while, they came up to a park bench and sat down. It was several minutes before any of them said anything.

"You know," said Wonk, "Fixer and Phat embody the political establishment, and as we suspected, these guys will never support anything that threatens the status quo."

For the next hour, the three friends debated the implications of what they had seen and heard.

"I think the Animals for Honest Government group was a little soft on us last night," Hedge said at one point. "Although the questions were tough, no one in the hall was threatened by our hedgie, so our ideas didn't get the scrutiny they needed. As a result, we clearly weren't prepared for the meeting with Fixer."

"Good point," said Wonk. "What should we do?"

"I have an idea," said Hedge after a brief pause. "What we really need to do is present our proposals to a large group that includes both rats who benefit from the status quo and ordinary animals like us. Imagine how quickly other animals will begin to support us once they see how the rats react, particularly if they react like Fixer did."

"How about the Freedom Forum?" asked Conn. "The annual meeting is in two weeks. What if we were to get Hedge on the Forum agenda? He'd be able to address thousands of animals all at once."

Freedom Forum started many years ago as a celebration of the Freedom Island Constitution and the freedoms it guarantees. Over time, though, it had evolved into a grandstanding and networking opportunity for elite politicians, civic leaders, and business owners. Despite being dominated by powerful and connected rats, many ordinary animals still made time to attend and participate.

"I thought the Forum agenda was pretty restricted," said Wonk.

"It is," replied Conn, "but I'll bet I can convince a few rat friends to put Hedge on the agenda."

"Sounds like a great idea!" said Hedge.

"Let's be careful about this," warned the professor. "I agree that you should present your ideas to the Forum, but the rats who control it will react negatively and maybe even aggressively once they realize what you're proposing, particularly since you'll be speaking in front of a huge and potentially very receptive crowd. You're not going to win any rat popularity contests."

"I don't expect to," replied Hedge. "The biggest group in the Forum audience will be the seventy percent of voters who aren't well-connected rats in the cheese. That's the group I want to address. That's the group that will support our hedgie, especially once they see how the rats react."

XI

Preparations for the Forum had been underway for some time. Organizers had been working for months to develop the agenda, arrange for speakers, and plan the festivities. Officials predicted a record turnout.

In addition to the usual speeches by various rats announcing big programs and costly investments, the Planning Committee decided to try something new by allotting time for a Good Government panel discussion. Reform Rat, who had been selected as Forum Director and head of the Planning Committee, believed that it would be politically valuable to showcase ideas for improving government efficiency and effectiveness. He not only convinced Committee members to approve the Good Government panel, but he also talked them into allowing him to handpick the panel participants. Perhaps it was merely a coincidence that Reform planned to run for Esteemed Leader during the next election.

The Forum agenda was a closely guarded secret. Each year, participants would eagerly await the opening ceremony, during which the Forum Director would announce the agenda and introduce the speakers. It was often the most entertaining part of the Forum, one that no animal wanted to miss.

Of course, the fact that the agenda was top secret didn't stop Conn from learning about it almost immediately. Rats are cunning but not to be trusted with confidential information.

The Good Government panel is the perfect venue for Hodge, thought Conn to himself as he read through a draft copy of the agenda he had procured from a friend of his on the Planning Committee. Unfortunately, panel members had already been chosen. Reform had selected Biz Rat, Rich Rat, Spotless Rat, and Fairness Rat as participants. He thought it was important for good government ideas to come from ordinary citizens rather than politicians. After all, what better way to promote democracy?

Conn knew Reform well. He and Hedge had helped Reform win his first election campaign for the Council. He thought he'd have a good chance at convincing Reform to somehow make room for Hedge on the panel.

"Conn, nice to see you," said Reform, who had agreed to meet Conn for lunch. "It's been too long! What can I do for you?"

"Thanks for visiting with me, Reform," replied Conn. "I'm hoping that you'll consider adding a seat on the Good Government panel."

"Maybe," said Reform. "Whom do you have in mind?"

"Hedge Hedgehog," replied Conn. He explained that Hedge had a lot of good ideas for the panel that would resonate with the audience.

Reform gave the proposal some thought and finally agreed to include Hedge on the panel. It was too bad that Reform didn't check first with Fixer Rat back at Council Headquarters.

***

"Good news," said Conn as he walked up to Hedge and Wonk, who were seated at a table thinking about the remarks Hedge might deliver if Conn were able to get him on the panel.

"What's up?" asked the professor.

"Reform Rat is serving as Forum Director this year," replied Conn. "He's organized a Good Government panel discussion for the afternoon session, and I've convinced him to include Hedge as a participant."

"Fantastic!" exclaimed Hedge. "Conn, you're a genius."

"Just out of curiosity," asked Wonk, "who else is on the panel?"

"Biz, Rich, Spotless, and Fairness, with Reform as the moderator," said Conn.

"Perfect," said Wonk. "What a great opportunity. I can't wait to see their reaction when Hedge presents our ideas."

"Let's hope it's civil," said Hedge.

***

The day for the Freedom Forum finally arrived. As usual, animals camped out nearby overnight, hoping to secure the best seats when the Forum grounds opened early the next morning. Hedge, Wonk, and Conn didn't arrive until just before the opening session. As a Good Government panel participant, Hedge had a front row seat and was able to invite Wonk and Conn to sit with him.

Reform Rat launched the proceedings with what he thought was a stirring speech. Animals applauded politely as he recounted the sacrifices he had endured as a public servant. Limited Party rats cheered wildly as he reminisced about the Council's accomplishments over the past year and the overall prosperity of Freedom Island, while the opposition Active Party rats sat in stone-faced silence.

Following his lengthy address, Reform revealed the Forum agenda. The morning session would be devoted to hearing political, civic, and business leaders announce various programs and investments, while the afternoon would be dedicated to a Good Government panel, which Reform himself would facilitate.

Once again, the Limited Party rats cheered, trying without success to get everyone to join in with the same enthusiasm.

"Reform Rat—Better government! Reform Rat—Better government!"

After a few minutes, the partisan cheering died down and the formal program began. Rat after rat stepped up to the platform to speak, each one trying to top the other with ambitious proposals, the cost of which didn't seem the least bit worrying.

"Biz Rat has done such a fabulous job with his meadow project," exclaimed one speaker. "We simply must convince him to embark on another. I propose doubling the Council's investments in meadow-related projects!"

"Fairness Rat can do so much more for Poor Church Mice," said another speaker. "Imagine how quickly we could end poverty if we really tried. I propose tripling the amount of cheese the Council devotes to helping the poor!"

"Spotless Rat is leading the way with Clean Island rules and regulations," said another. "He wants unlimited authority to go even further. How can the Council deny him?"

Soon, it was time for lunch. Rich Rat had underwritten the entire event, and all the tables were piled high with cheese he had supplied. Council subsidies and tax breaks had enabled him to become the largest cheese owner on Freedom Island.

"Friends," announced Reform as everyone finished lunch, "I'd like to resume our program by introducing participants in this afternoon's Good Government panel discussion. We're extremely fortunate to have with us today Biz Rat, Rich Rat, Spotless Rat, and Fairness Rat, whom you all know and admire."

Cheers and whistles from the Limited and Active Party rats punctuated the crowd's polite applause.

"We have one other panel member you may not know but who is sure to have some interesting things to say. Please welcome Hedge Hedgehog."

The crowd applauded mildly, not really knowing how to react. Conn and Wonk offered the only real enthusiasm.

Fixer Rat had been standing off to the side near the platform. He was lending a hand behind the scenes so that everything would go smoothly. He couldn't see the panel members, but he could hear Reform making the introductions.

"Hedge is on the Good Government panel?" exclaimed Fixer to himself as Reform finished introducing Hedge. *Oh no!* he thought, remembering the ideas Hedge had presented to him in his office several days before. *How did he get on the panel? This is going to be a disaster!*

Fixer ran out to the front of the platform and tried to signal Reform. But it was too late. The panel members had already taken their seats. Reform didn't see Fixer's frantic waving anyway.

"Let's get started," said Reform. "Hedge, you're the newest face up here, would you care to kick things off? What ideas do you have to promote good government?"

"Thank you, Reform," said Hedge as he stepped over to the podium. Fixer buried his face in his paws.

"Watch this," whispered Conn to Wonk.

"My fellow citizens," began Hedge. "I have some new ideas to safeguard freedom and prosperity for Freedom Island. They're different than what you usually hear, so brace yourselves."

The other panel members looked at each other. The crowd fell completely silent.

Hedge pulled out the remarks he had written with Wonk's help and loudly tore them up.

"I had prepared some notes for my brief talk," he continued, "but I think I'm going to speak to you from the heart instead."

Hedge paused. No one moved.

"Let's reflect for a moment on what we've heard today," he stated in a loud and clear voice. "What we've heard sounds like pretty good news. According to Reform Rat, Freedom Island is in great shape. And according to the proposals offered by other speakers, there's no shortage of good government coming our way."

The crowd remained silent.

"Now, hold on a minute," continued Hedge. "I've just recapped all this great news and not one of you is cheering. And I think I know why. It's because beneath the surface of all this good news, you know that something bad is going on. For every program they mention, you know there's rampant corruption. For every benefit they promise, you know that the costs are much higher than they should be due to waste and abuse. For every plan they propose, you know that the resulting increased tax burden will be both convoluted and unfairly distributed.

"But here's what's really frustrating you," continued Hedge. "You know these rats are in the cheese, yet you feel powerless to do anything about it because nothing you've tried in an attempt to stop them seems to work. You supported the Active Party, and those rats got into the cheese. You then supported the Limited Party, and those rats got into the cheese despite promises not to. Frankly, as evidenced by the presentations you heard earlier today, rats from both parties are into so much cheese for themselves and their supporters that it no longer matters to ordinary animals who controls the Council."

The crowd grew restless. One irate porcupine suddenly stood up. "Why has this happened?" she shouted.

"I'll tell you why," replied Hedge. "It has happened because, over time, the rats have conspired to weaken the one force that can keep them in check. And that's you, the voters. They've done this with deficit spending, hiding the cost of what they're doing by deferring it to future generations. They've done this by complicating the tax code so that when you do pay taxes, you can't really understand what you're paying and how it's linked to all this spending."

The crowd booed loudly.

"But that's not the worst of it," thundered Hedge. "These rats have realized that there's a little rat in every animal, so they've conspired to addict all of you to some of their spending and taxing schemes. How many of you feel like you're entitled to a special tax deduction that the rats have provided, or to a special spending program they've organized? By making you feel dependent on the system, they've minimized the risk that you'll get upset when the rest of the system gets out of control.

They know you'll be happy so long as your particular benefit remains undisturbed."

The crowd grew quiet again, with everyone realizing that they had been complicit in the rats' scheming.

"Deep down," continued Hedge, "you know this can't continue. You know that unchecked, the rats will consume more and more cheese until the very foundations of Freedom Island are threatened. The time to act is now, and I believe I have a plan that will work."

By this point, the political rats in the audience had grown angry. Off to the side, several Limited Party rats approached Fixer Rat, who was frantically pacing back and forth, trying to think of a way to get Hedge off the platform. As they began to conspire with Fixer, some Active Party rats heard the conversation and joined in. For once, Fixer was attracting bipartisan cooperation.

"Hedge is crazy," Fixer said as they huddled. "We have to stop him. If he talks much longer, the crowds are going to chase us all off the island."

"So what do we do?" asked one really big rat. Actually, they were all really big rats.

"I have an idea," said Fixer. He hunkered down with the other rats and began to lay out a plan.

The rats on the panel were unhappy about Hedge, too. Biz, Spotless, and Fairness stood up from their seats, clearly upset. Rich Rat simply stormed off the stage in a huff. Reform Rat, sensing that he was about to lose control of the proceedings, tried to calm everyone down.

"Thanks, Hedge," he offered weakly. "That was lovely. Why don't we move on?"

"I'm not done," said Hedge firmly.

"I think you are," said Biz moving across the platform. He stepped in front of Hedge, shoved him aside, and began to address the audience himself.

"Animals" shouted Biz above the growing noise level, "Hedge has lost his mind. He's criticizing our very form of government. Don't let him fill your heads with these lies. I certainly don't believe him, and neither should you!"

"You're wrong!" shouted several animals in the crowd. "Let him continue!"

Hedge walked back up to Biz and did a little shoving himself, returning to the podium. The crowd cheered as he did.

"As I said," he continued, even more forcefully than before, "I believe I have a plan that will restore integrity and efficiency to our government."

The crowd began to chant. "We want Hedge—we want Hedge!"

"We hedgehogs have always had a natural defense against predators," continued Hedge. "When attacked, we can protect ourselves from injury by snapping into a spiny ball. We call this defensive mechanism a hedgie, and I think this same idea can be used to keep the rats out of the cheese. Who here would like to get stuck by one of my spines?"

Hedge raised his paws to reveal how long and sharp his spines truly were.

"Not us!" cried the crowd.

"Now, how can a hedgie help us get the rats out of the cheese?" Hedge asked. "Well, I'll tell you. As I mentioned, the rats have conspired to weaken you, the voters. You need a hedgie, a defensive mechanism to stop them cold and restore your voting strength at election time. Only you, the voters, can keep the rats out of the cheese."

"Tell us more!" shouted the crowd.

"OK," said Hedge. "In my view, we need a hedgie with three interlocking elements. First, we need a Freedom Rule that requires cheese spending to be matched by cheese taxes. With this rule, we'll be sure that rats can't hide the fact that they're in the cheese. Second, we need a single rate cheese income tax applied equally to the top 85% of income earners. Replacing current taxes with this new tax will ensure that when the rats spend more to get into the cheese, all taxpayers will be equally affected and will thus be motivated to speak with a unified voice at election time. Third and last, we need an asset tax, which will ensure that the truly rich who avoid or are exempt from taxes now will contribute to the tax burden."

Hedge spoke carefully and slowly, pausing for emphasis after describing each element. The crowd listened intently, remaining silent as Hedge explained everything.

"Now, I know this will take some time to absorb and understand," he continued. "But keep in mind the overall theme of what I'm saying. The rats are in the cheese, and our freedom and prosperity are in danger as a result. They're in the cheese because they've weakened the one force that can keep them out, the voters. We need this hedgie to restore voter strength. If we can unite and accomplish this, we can put Freedom Island back on a sound footing for us and our posterity."

The crowd literally exploded. It was the first time they had heard someone speak so clearly and compellingly about the problems they faced on Freedom Island. It was also the first time someone had offered an honest and promising solution to these problems, one that focused on empowering voters and not the well-connected rats.

Not surprisingly, the rats didn't find much to like in what Hedge said, either in his indictment of the rats or, especially, in his proposed solution. Hedge had struck directly at the rats and their cheese connection.

"Hedge is wrong!" shouted Fairness Rat to the crowd as she shoved Hedge aside. "Poor Church Mice will suffer if we adopt his ideas! And he's going to destroy our retirement security!"

Hedge tried to regain center stage, but Spotless Rat pushed him as he tried, knocking him off the platform. "Hedge lies!" he shouted. "His silly ideas will threaten our environment! Are we going to let Hedge allow polluters to destroy Freedom Island?"

The noise from the crowd reached a fevered pitch, with rats and other animals shouting back and forth at each other. Several fights broke out.

"You don't want to listen to Hedge!" shouted Biz Rat again. "He's a failed business owner! He couldn't even keep his store open! If we adopt his proposals, we'll condemn Freedom Island to the same failure!"

The fighting grew in intensity. With help from Wonk and Conn, Hedge climbed back up on the platform and tried to address the crowd. One of rats in the audience bit Wonk viciously as he helped Hedge, calling him a traitor to all rats. The aging Wonk cried out in pain and fell back from the stage.

"Friends, calm yourselves!" shouted Hedge as he returned to the podium. "It's clear we have disagreements, but we must discuss our differences in a civil manner!"

Meanwhile, Fixer was just about ready to set in motion his plan to get Hedge off the platform and away from the Forum. Quickly, the rats who had conspired with him took their places around the stage, with Active Party rats on the left side and Limited Party rats on the right. With a quick signal from Fixer, they moved up onto the platform all at once. Snarling and bearing their teeth, they charged toward Hedge.

Hedge looked nervously at the approaching rats. He knew he was in trouble. He knew that if he didn't do something fast, he might not get off the stage in one piece.

It happened so quickly.

With mortal danger approaching, Hedge's reflexes took over and he snapped into the shape of a ball, his sharp spines protruding out in every direction.

In that instant, everything came to a standstill. The marauding rats stopped in their tracks. The fighting on the platform came to a halt. The brawling in the audience ceased. The shouts subsided. Soon, there was total silence as everyone focused on the spiny ball before them, the sun reflecting off its razor-sharp points.

After a few minutes, Hedge peeked out. Seeing no danger, he unrolled from his hedgie and stepped back up to the podium.

"Fellow citizens," he stated calmly, "I believe I've made my point. A hedgie *can* keep the rats out of the cheese. The next step is up to you."

Hedge turned and slowly walked off the platform, down the center aisle, and away from the Forum. No one said a word, and no one followed him, not even Conn, who had stayed behind to help care for the injured Wonk.

Hedge meandered across a meadow and through the town square. After a while, as he had done many times in the past, he decided to go down to the river. The water had a calming effect on him. As he listened, he began to feel better.

XII

"edge," came a voice from behind. Hedge had been sitting by the river for some time contemplating what had happened. Hedge turned around, startled to see Politico Rat standing in front of him.

"Pol?" exclaimed Hedge. He hadn't seen or heard from Pol in the years since Pol was defeated for reelection to the Council. "What are you doing here?"

"I've come to tell you that you're right," responded Pol.

"About what?" said Hedge.

"About everything you said at the Forum today," replied Pol. "You have a keen understanding of what's wrong on Freedom Island, and I think your solutions, once they're developed, have a good chance of solving these problems. I know I failed you before, but I want to help you save our island. I want to help you save us from ourselves."

"I'm not so sure I've done anything worthwhile," said Hedge. "Look at the carnage I caused. All that violence. Plus, Wonk was injured. I don't even know if he's OK."

"Why don't you come with me back to town," said Pol. "There's something I think you'll want to see."

Grudgingly, Hedge agreed to go. After a while, they arrived back in town. As Hedge and Pol turned a corner, they saw the town square and the Freedom Rules Monument. More importantly, they saw a huge crowd of animals.

"What's going on?" asked Hedge a little nervously, mindful of the many rats who wanted him silenced, or worse.

"All of these animals have come from the Forum," replied Pol. "Your words struck a chord with them, and they're here to encourage you. You should go to them, hear them, and speak to them."

Hedge stood there for a few moments. Slowly, he began to make his way to the square. As he did, one animal spotted him. It was Nutsy Squirrel, now one of Hedge's biggest fans.

"There he is!" shouted Nutsy.

The crowd erupted as soon as Nutsy spoke.

"We want Hedge—we want Hedge!"

Hedge strode down to the square amid the chants. Just as the sun was setting, he stepped up onto a platform in front of the Freedom Rules monument. Before him, thousands of animals cheered enthusiastically. A feeling of pride welled up in Hedge like he had never felt before.

"Hedge," said a voice behind him on the platform. Startled, Hedge turned and saw that Pol had followed him down to the square.

"These animals believe in you, and they want to help make your ideas a reality," said Pol, who then stepped down from the platform so Hedge could speak.

"Friends," Hedge began, "I'm overwhelmed." He choked up a little as he noticed Conn and Wonk down in front. Wonk's injuries were thankfully minor.

Hedge realized that about seventy percent of the Forum audience had made its way to the square, leaving nearly all the rats behind. It was the group he thought would support his ideas anyway. Regaining his composure, Hedge turned to the crowd.

"You've demonstrated great personal initiative in coming here today," shouted Hedge. "Not just because it's a long walk from the Forum…"

Laughter rang through the square.

"…but because deep down, you know that we face some serious problems and that you can and should be part of the solution."

The crowd roared with approval.

"Now, restoring integrity and efficiency in our government through the hedgie I propose will not be easy," continued Hedge. "It's our collective fault that we've allowed the rats to get in the cheese, so it's going to take our collective action to solve the problem."

Hedge paused. The crowd grew silent.

"Probably the toughest thing to accept is that collective success will mean individual sacrifice. As we move forward, there will be winners and losers. Some of you will come out ahead economically, some will not. If we're going to make this work, those of us who end up disadvantaged must not lose faith in our overall objective. If no one were willing to accept personal sacrifice, or accept loss in the face of another's gain, we would never get anywhere; we would never restore our freedoms.

"Second," Hedge continued, "the special benefits and provisions we all take advantage of in the tax code were placed there to addict us to the current system, and giving them up will be difficult. But if we can work through this pain, we'll be rewarded with a tax system defined by fairness, equity and consistency.

"Third," said Hedge, "we have to take the long road. Only through carefully crafted amendments to our Freedom Rules, which will take time to develop, can we create a legal framework strong enough to keep the rats, and all animals, out of the cheese. A few quick-fix rules, or a couple of laws here and there, won't be sufficient. The challenge we face is much bigger. We must create something that protects us from ourselves.

"Lastly," said Hedge, "we must be strong. The rats will resist our efforts, and they'll do so with unimaginable vigor, persistence and creativity. Neither political party will support us. No major business, union, charitable, or media group will support us. The change we seek will have to come from us directly. As a result, we're going to have to work hard to encourage, to convince, and to inspire our fellow citizens to act for the common good. Because only when we do the right thing collectively can we truly prosper individually."

"If the current parties won't support us, why don't we form a new political party?" shouted one animal.

"That's a great suggestion," shouted another. "We can call it the Hedgehog Party!"

"Not a bad idea," said Hedge, chuckling as the crowd roared with approval. "With your help, we can use this new party as a vehicle for spreading the word about our ideas across Freedom Island."

"Disconnect the well-connected rats!" yelled one animal. "Let's get those dirty rats and send them packing!" screamed another.

"No!" shouted Hedge when he heard these remarks. "Blaming the rats is the first thing to avoid."

The crowd quickly grew quiet.

"It's true that the rats have gone further than most in exploiting our common weakness for cheese," continued Hedge, "but in truth we've *all* gotten into the cheese to some extent, so it's dishonest to blame only the rats. Besides, blaming others gets us no closer to a solution and only distracts us from building the unity we'll need to succeed."

The crowd cheered and whistled as Hedge spoke.

"I think I've said all I need to for now," declared Hedge as he concluded his talk, "but before I go, let me thank you for coming from the Forum today. Now let's unite as members of the Hedgehog Party to spread hope and goodwill. Tell everyone you meet about what we propose and why. Let all animals know that, with their help, we can solve the problems we face. We won't change the Council or its politics overnight, but in time we will bring about change, and change for the better.

"And remember," shouted Hedge as he raised his paws. "We must come together now! We must move forward now! We must act now! And why?"

The crowd knew the words to yell in response.

"The rats are in the cheese!"

***

Not far from the town square was a row of bushes and trees, planted by the Council to commemorate some long-forgotten event. Anyone sitting amidst this splendid greenery had an excellent view of the town square.

"They're going to ruin one of the greatest cheese-thieving schemes in animal history," moaned Phat Mouse. "There will always be rats in the cheese, but I'm going to have to settle for a much smaller cut now."

He and Fixer Rat had secretly followed the crowd of animals who left the Forum in search of Hedge. From their vantage point, they had heard Hedge's speech and the deafening applause.

"The party's over for us. We're through," said Phat angrily.

Fixer scowled as he listened to Phat.

"Not if I have anything to say about it," he snarled.

***

"Hedge," shouted Conn as he and Wonk walked up to where Hedge was greeting noisy well-wishers after wrapping up his speech. "Someone told me that Fixer and Phat are sitting up under the Council trees along that ridge over there."

"I'll bet they've already started plotting against us," said Wonk.

"No doubt," replied Hedge calmly. He paused briefly to survey the still-cheering crowd.

"Bring 'em on. We're ready for whatever they've got."

Made in the USA
Charleston, SC
24 August 2010